ARCO

W9-BQW-193

Everything you need to score high

TOEFL*
Grammar Workbook

3rd Edition

Phyllis L. Lim
Mary Kurtin
Laurie Wellman, Consulting Editor

MACMILLAN • USA

Third Edition

Macmillan General Reference
A Simon & Schuster Macmillan Company
1633 Broadway
New York NY 10019-6785

Macmillan Publishing books may be purchased for business or
sales promotional use. For information, please write: Special
Markets Department, Macmillan Publishing USA, 1633 Broadway,
New York, NY 10019.

An ARCO Book

MACMILLAN is a registered trademark of Macmillan, Inc.
ARCO is a registered trademark of Prentice-Hall, Inc.

ISBN: 0-02-862464-5

Manufactured in the United States of America

10 9 8 7 6 5 4 3 2

CONTENTS

International Students' Guide to College Admissions

By Anna Leider, President, Octameron Associates

Getting into an American College

Students making plans to study abroad often choose to study in the United States. The reason is clear. The U.S. education system has developed in response to the needs of a diverse population, and is therefore adaptable to many career and personal goals. At the same time, students should keep in mind that college-level study in the U.S. is both serious and demanding, especially for international students who come without family or cultural support. Accordingly, before students decide to study in the U.S., they should ask themselves the following:

1. Why do I want to study in the U.S.? Is the program of study I plan to pursue not available in my own country? Am I truly committed to education, or am I just trying to avoid an unpleasant home situation?

2. What do I want to study? Am I studying something relevant to my country's needs? What will my degree be worth when I return home?

3. How well prepared am I? Have I completed the equivalent of a high school education? How proficient am I in English?

4. What is my financial status? Will I be able to support myself if I am unable to work while in the U.S.?

5. Am I mature enough to live in a different culture? Am I accepting of different customs, food and climate? Am I ready to be looked on as "a foreigner?"

If, after thinking about all these questions, a student still wants to pursue a U.S. education, he or she should begin the application process.

International Student Characteristics

Nearly 356,000 international students currently study in the U.S. The largest group (approximately 180,540) comes from South or East Asia. Sixty-eight percent of international students are male. Eighty-eight percent attend four-year colleges and universities. Sixty-five percent attend public institutions. Twenty-one percent of international students study engineering. Twenty percent study business or management. Thirty-eight and a half percent are working toward a four-year undergraduate degree. Forty-four percent are working toward a graduate degree. Eleven percent are working toward a two-year associate degree. The remaining six-and-a-half percent are in non-degree programs, or English language programs.

Choosing a College

Choosing a college from among 3,000 options is not easy for anyone, but the process is especially difficult for students unfamiliar with the U.S. This section is intended to supplement the general chapter on college selection. It focuses on ways to begin researching colleges, and lists additional criteria for international students to consider as they read through brochures and college catalogs.

Overseas Educational Advising Centers. These agencies are the best places for students to begin their research. Trained counselors are available to answer questions and provide guidance. The centers usually have books and catalogs with detailed information on study programs, application procedures, attendance costs and freshman class profiles. Overseas Counseling Centers sometimes contain videotapes of college campuses, so students can "visit" a variety of schools. A list of Overseas Educational Advising Centers is available from the College Board, Office of International Education, 1717 Massachusetts Avenue NW, Washington DC 20036, U.S.A.

Foreign Student Information Clearinghouse (FSIC). Many overseas counseling centers use this computer program to help students identify suitable colleges. The student answers a series of questions about school preferences and in return, receives a computer printout of schools meeting his or her requirements. A small fee is charged for this service. Students should discuss the institutions named on the printout with a college advisor, and write the schools directly for more current information. Please note: Use of the Clearinghouse does not mean students have been admitted to the colleges listed on their printout! More information on FSIC may be obtained from the College Board (address above).

Field of Study. Unless students know exactly what they want to study, they should select a school that offers a wide range of subjects.

Location. In selecting a college, students must consider geography, climate, and demographics. No matter what their preference, they will discover a school. Colleges are found near beaches, mountains, and deserts; in regions that have freezing temperatures for nearly half the year, and in regions that are always warm; in densely populated cities and in thinly populated rural areas. Note: Large cities are generally more ethnically diverse and offer a greater variety of cultural activities.

Size of School. Students must also choose between a large university and a small college. A large university generally has better international student support services; a small school is often less intimidating.

Accreditation. Unlike many countries, the U.S. has no centralized authority for educational matters. Instead, it uses a system of accreditation to verify the quality of institutions. Accreditation covers admission and graduation requirements, curriculum, and academic facilities. To enroll in a non-accredited program is usually a waste of time and money. All of the schools listed in this book are accredited.

Inquiry Process

After students have narrowed their choice of schools to ten or twelve, they should write to the schools directly to obtain application forms, current catalogs, and information on international student services.

Letter of Inquiry. The inquiry letter should include the following:

1. Full name, age, marital status, and mailing address.

2. Education to date (include the location of the school, subjects studied, dates of attendance, class rank, and grades received).

3. Total amount and source of funds (in U.S. dollars) which will be available to contribute to education each year.

4. Planned course of study.

5. Estimate of English proficiency (written and spoken).

International Student Advisor. Almost all schools with international students have at least one designated international student advisor. This person helps students make cultural, academic, and social adjustments. He or she can answer questions about visas, financial assistance, student employment, and U.S. government regulations specific to the international student community. Finally, the advisor can help students find places to stay during semester breaks (small schools, especially, close down between semesters and often will not allow any students to remain on campus).

English as a Second Language (ESL). This program is designed to help students improve their written and spoken English. Many schools will accept students not fluent in English with the understanding they will complete an ESL program before they begin their official program of study. *English Language and Orientation Programs in the United States* contains a list of ESL programs (the book is available from the Institute of International Education (I.I.E.), 809 United Nations Plaza, New York, NY 10017, U.S.A.). Note: These are not degree programs, so it does not matter if they are accredited. In fact, very few are.

International Student Orientation. Some schools have a special orientation for international students before the start of the fall semester. This is a good time for students to become familiar with the school and the surrounding community, to meet the international student advisor, and to meet each other.

Community Support Programs. Large cities, especially, will have non-profit organizations that sponsor activities for international students. Activities include tours of the city and surrounding areas, museum visits, travel seminars, "ethnic" dinners, and visits with American families.

Mailing Instructions. Although it is expensive, students should use air mail for all their correspondence. Students should also send colleges the correct international air postage (which may be purchased in local post offices) so their requests are answered using air mail. Why is this so important? Surface mail takes months to reach a location abroad and students may miss deadlines while waiting for their ship to come in.

Applying to Colleges

In filling out the college application, students should be completely honest and not omit anything. An incomplete application, or one with deliberate falsehoods, will be returned and the student may miss application deadlines or be denied admission altogether. If students must leave something unanswered, they should attach a note which explains the reason. Students may be asked to do any or all of the following.

Complete an Application Form. The application form is used to collect basic information about the applicant, including country of citizenship, community or scholastic awards, future goals, employment history, and statement of personal objectives.

Pay an Application Fee. In countries with a currency restriction in effect, this fee (usually between U.S.$10 and U.S.$50) may be waived.

Submit a Transcript. Students must provide an official English language transcript (a detailed list of subjects studied, examination results, and an explanation of the school's grading system). Official transcripts are those sent directly by one school to another, and are stamped with an official school seal.

Submit Letters of Recommendation. Letters must be from teachers or employers and should discuss the applicant's strengths and weaknesses as a candidate for admission to a U.S. college.

Take Standardized Tests. Many schools require students to take the SAT or the ACT. Test scores must be submitted by the testing agency directly to the schools designated by the applicant.

Demonstrate English Language Proficiency. Students must submit satisfactory test results from an examination such as the Test of English as a Foreign Language (TOEFL). The TOEFL is a timed examination consisting of listening comprehension, written expression, and reading comprehension. The TOEFL Bulletin of Information contains registration forms, a list of test centers, test dates, and sample questions. To obtain a bulletin, write TOEFL, Box 6151, Princeton, New Jersey 08541–6151, U.S.A. Reminder: The TOEFL is not an application for admission to any institution. Two other English language proficiency tests are the American Language Institute of Georgetown University (ALIGU) exam which is given by American Embassies overseas, and the Michigan Test (English Language Institute, University of Michigan, Ann Arbor, Michigan 48104, U.S.A.) Students should check with the schools to which they are applying to learn which tests to take. Many schools recognize only TOEFL scores.

Submit Detailed Financial Information. Students must fill out the College Scholarship Service's "Declaration and Certification of Finances" (or its equivalent) to prove they will have adequate financial support for the intended period of study. All sources of support must be documented. Savings accounts must be verified with financial statements signed by a bank official. Sponsors, whether they be employers, relatives, or friends, must sign an affidavit of support witnessed by a Notary Public or Legal Official. If the student lives in a country that restricts funds sent abroad, the student must submit bank approval for currency exchange (a guarantee that funds will be transferred to the U.S. college or university).

Certification of Health. Students must fill out a medical history form. In addition, students are often given a brief medical examination upon arrival at the school. Note: Health care in the U.S. is very expensive. As students are likely to require health care at some point during their college years, they are strongly encouraged to protect themselves by enrolling in the school's health insurance plan.

Paying for College

Employment. Strict regulations govern the employment of international students in the U.S., therefore, students should not assume they will have a salary to assist them in paying their educational expenses. International students are eligible for fellowships and assistantships but, returning students and graduate students are given preference for these positions.

Grants and Loans. Students should not expect to receive money from U.S. government student aid programs. This money is reserved for U.S. citizens or permanent residents. Private banks may extend personal loans to students with the necessary collateral.

Scholarships. Some institutions offer scholarships to entering international students. They want to attract outstanding students from all across the world, to diversify their student body and enhance their reputation. For a list of scholarships, get *Scholarships for International Students: A Guide to U.S.A. Colleges and Universities* from Scholarship Research Group, 16600 Sprague Road, Ste. 110, Middleburg Heights, Ohio 44130.

Private Sources. Many private awards are available for study and research. For information on these awards, write to the I.I.E. (address above) and ask for *Financial Resources for International Study.* Information on Fulbright Hayes awards (a large scholarship program) is available from Binational Education Centers.

Visa and Immigration Requirements

Visa and immigration requirements are complex. A brief summary of the most common travel documents follows. For additional information, or clarification, students should contact a U.S. consulate.

Passport. Students must have a passport! This document is issued to students by their home government to identify them for the purpose of traveling to other countries. Passports are official documents and may be used only by the person to whom they are issued. Passports should never be lent to anyone. They should never be used as a form of collateral, nor should they ever be altered, except by authorized government agents.

Visa. This is a stamp on a passport that gives people permission to enter a country other than their own. Issuance of a student visa requires a valid passport, proof of English language proficiency, and proof of financial support. More specific requirements are listed for each visa type.

F-1. Nonimmigrant Student Visa. This is the most common visa granted to students. An F-1 visa permits students to enter the U.S. temporarily to pursue a full-time program of study. An F-1 visa is issued only after receipt of a Form I-20A, Certificate of Eligibility for Nonimmigrant Student Status. Form I-20A is sent to students by a school after they have been accepted. It indicates the program name and cost, the expected term of study, verification of English proficiency, and the student's means of financial support. Students must apply for their visa using the I-20A issued by the school they plan to attend, and no other. U.S. Government regulations require attendance for at least one semester at the school whose I-20 is used to obtain a visa. Form I-20A (like Forms I-20M and IAP-66 described below) will be returned to the student after the visa has been issued. Students should be careful not to lose it, as they must present the form at the port of entry when they arrive in the U.S.

M-1. New Student Visa. This classification of student visa is granted to students who wish to pursue a vocational program of study. The visa requirements are similar to F-1 visas, except the visa is issued for a shorter period of time and form I-20A is replaced by Form I-20M.

J-1. Exchange Visitor Visa. This visa is granted to students or teachers participating in an educational exchange program recognized by the U.S. Department of State. Generally, these are people engaged in research, consultation, teaching, or specialized training. A visa is issued only after receipt of Form IAP-66, Certificate of Eligibility for Exchange Visitor Status. This form is similar to the I-20A, except it is issued by the U.S. organization or government agency sponsoring the student.

F-2, M-2, J-2 Dependent Visas. These visas are granted to the spouse and children of F-1, M-1, and J-1 visa recipients, respectively.

Form I-94, Arrival-Departure Record. This is a U.S. Immigration form that indicates the purpose of the student's admission to the U.S., and the length of time the student may remain. Form I-94 should remain with the student's passport.

Form I-20 ID. This yellow card describes the entitlements F-1 or M-1 students may receive, such as whether they may accept employment or transfer schools. It also bears an 11-digit identification number assigned to the student (for life) by the INS. Students should keep this card separate from their passport, and carry it with them at all times. Thy should also memorize their ID number in case the card is lost or stolen. Replacement will be much easier.

Employment. An F-1 student may accept part-time (less than 20 hours per week) on-campus employment while school is in session, but these jobs are generally low-paying ($3.00 to $6.00 per hour) relative to student expenses. Full-time work is permitted only during vacations. Off-campus employment is permitted only with approval of the Immigration and Naturalization Service (INS), and that approval is extremely difficult to obtain. The spouse of an F-1 student is not eligible to work under any conditions. Neither M-1 students nor their spouses may accept employment of any kind. J-1 students may work either on- or off-campus provided they can show financial need and they obtain the approval of their program sponsor. Spouses of J-1 students may receive permission to work from the INS if they can prove employment is needed for their own support (or the support of a child). The spouse may not work if the wages are for the support of a J-1 student.

Change of Schools. F-1 students may transfer from one school to another to begin a new educational program only with INS permission. F-1 students may transfer from one school to another to pursue the same educational program just by notifying the INS a transfer has occurred. M-1 students may not change their educational objectives. They may not transfer between schools after six months. And they may not switch their student status to F-1. J-1 students may transfer between schools or programs as long as they have approval from their program sponsor.

Intent to Return Home. Students should not expect their student status to lead to an immigrant visa. In fact, students who do not intend to return home after finishing their studies are legally barred from even obtaining a student visa. In the visa interview, the U.S. consul will want to hear about close family ties and job options available at home upon completion of studies.

Tourist (B-2) Visas. Students should not come to the U.S. on a tourist visa and expect to change their classification after arrival. The INS is strict about this. Students who want to visit the United States before their student visa can be processed should prove to the U.S. consul their intent (and financial ability) to attend one of the schools to which they've applied. The consul realizes some students may want to look at schools before deciding which one to attend, and can stamp "prospective student" on a B-2 visa. This will eliminate later problems with the INS.

Arrival in the United States

Students should plan to arrive on a weekday when college and university offices are open and staff is available to assist them. Some schools (those located near ports of entry) may send representatives to the airport to assist students with immigration procedures.

Welcome, and best of luck!

Some of the material contained in these pages has been condensed from *Scholarships for International Students: A Guide to U.S.A. Colleges and Universities.* It is used by permission of Octameron Press.

Anna Leider is the owner and president of Octameron Associates, a publishing firm in the Washington, D.C. area that specializes in books on the topic of financial aid. Their publications cover the full range of financial aid available, from government grants to loans to private subsidies and scholarships.

I

WHAT IS THE TOEFL?

The TOEFL (Test of English as a Foreign Language) is a standardized test of English proficiency published by Educational Testing Service in Princeton, New Jersey, U.S.A. This test is used by many American and Canadian colleges and universities as part of admission requirements for foreign students whose native language is not English.

It is the student's responsibility to find out the admission requirements of any schools that he or she might apply to for admission. If the TOEFL is required, a student should plan on taking the TOEFL as soon as possible to allow time for these schools to receive and evaluate his or her scores. A "Bulletin of Information and Application Form" can be obtained free of charge by writing to the following address:

Test of English as a Foreign Language
Box 6151
Princeton, NJ 08541
U.S.A.

This bulletin contains an application form and detailed information on 1) where tests are administered; 2) when, where, and how to apply for the TOEFL; 3) what kind of identification is needed for the day of the test; and 4) how and when test scores are received. The bulletin attempts to anticipate and answer any questions a student may have about the test and how to apply to take it. He or she should read this bulletin carefully before filling out the application form. After applying for the TOEFL, each applicant will receive a ticket of confirmation and a "Handbook for Examinees." These will arrive about a month before the test is scheduled. The handbook will contain detailed information about the uses of score results. There is no one "passing" score for the TOEFL: Each college or university has its own policy. The TOEFL is only one factor considered in determining admission to a particular institution. Of course, every student wants to do as well as possible on the TOEFL and should use every opportunity to improve his or her English in general.

II

FORMAT OF THE *STRUCTURE AND WRITTEN EXPRESSION* SECTION OF THE TOEFL

The TOEFL has three sections:

1. Listening Comprehension

2. Structure and Written Expression

   Completion
   Correction
   (See below for Examples and Explanations)

3. Vocabulary and Reading Comprehension

This book deals only with the *Structure and Written Expression* section of the TOEFL. This section is designed to test your knowledge of standard written English. There are two parts to this section of the test, with separate directions for each.

Directions for the first part will be approximately as follows:

DIRECTIONS: Each of the following sentences is incomplete. Four words or phrases marked (A), (B), (C), and (D) are found under each sentence. Select the *one* word or phrase that *best* completes the sentence. Find the number of the problem on your answer sheet and mark your answer.

Example: If I _____ John, I will give him your mes-

sage.   **Sample Answer**

Ⓐ Ⓑ Ⓒ Ⓓ

(A) saw
(B) see
(C) would see
(D) will see

EXPLANATION: In standard written English, the sentence should read, "If I see John, I will give him your message." Therefore, you should have chosen (B).

Directions for the second part will be approximately as follows:

DIRECTIONS: In each of the following sentences, four words or phrases are underlined. These underlined parts are marked (A), (B), (C), and (D). Find the *one* underlined word or phrase that should be corrected or rewritten. Find the number of the problem on the answer sheet and mark your answer.

Example: Each of the students <u>were asked</u> <u>to be</u> <u>on</u> time for

A   B   C

class <u>on</u> Friday.   **Sample Answer**

D   Ⓐ Ⓑ Ⓒ Ⓓ

EXPLANATION: Answer (A) is not acceptable in standard written English. The subject of the verb is *Each,* which is singular. The verb should be *was asked.* Therefore, the sentence should read, "Each of the students was asked to be on time for class on Friday." You should have chosen (A) as the correct answer.

III

WHY USE THIS BOOK?

There are several features in this workbook that make it an excellent and efficient tool for preparing for the *Structure and Written Expression* section of the TOEFL.

First is the advantage of having a diagnostic test at the beginning of the book. Students may take this test as they start studying for the TOEFL 1) to get a picture of their ability in the *Structure and Written Expression* section, and 2) to pinpoint their strengths and weaknesses in grammar, enabling them to go straight to the parts of the book that offer practice in the areas where they have the most difficulty.

Second, this book has been designed to teach and simplify complex grammar as well as to give the student practice with questions similar to those on the actual TOEFL. This book contains grammatical explanations followed by simple correct-incorrect exercises that help students recognize and master one point of grammar at a time. There are chapter quizzes that test all points covered in one chapter. These quizzes follow the TOEFL format as much as possible. Then there are more difficult practice tests at the end of the book that contain grammar questions from the entire book. These are in TOEFL format. All exercises, quizzes, and practice TOEFL tests are keyed to specific points of grammar and the exact pages in this book where this material may be found.

IV

TIPS FOR TOEFL TAKERS

Plan your study schedule several weeks before the actual test. Don't expect to learn all the information in a few days. Study regularly. Here are some important points to remember when you take the TOEFL:

1. Keep track of the time. Take a watch or observe the time being posted on a blackboard in the room. Budget your time accordingly.

2. Guess if you do not know the answer. It will not count against you. No points are deducted from your score for incorrect answers. Your score is based on the number of questions you answer correctly. Therefore, you should answer every question. Fill in any questions you have left blank.

3. Follow all spoken and written directions to each section carefully.

4. Be careful to fill in each circle on the answer sheet completely. (The computer may not record your answer if the circle is not totally filled in.) Be sure not to fill in two answers for the same question.

5. Choose the *best* answer. Do not forget that more than one answer may appear grammatically correct, but only one will be the *best* choice.

6. Do the questions you are sure about first and then go back and check the ones you have not answered.

7. Choose the answer that seems clearest and most concise.

8. Work as quickly as you can, but do not be careless.

SEVEN STEPS TO USING THIS BOOK SUCCESSFULLY

1. Take the Diagnostic Test.

2. Check your answers with the error key following the test.
    The error key gives the name of the grammatical point covered and the page number where review material can be found.

3. Study the specific grammatical points carefully.
    Do the exercise that follows each one. Check your answers with the error key, which refers you to a specific grammatical rule or note. In some cases, *but not in all*, the error keys contain more than one possible corrected answer. The error keys are located at the end of each chapter.

4. Take the chapter quizzes.
    Check your answers with the error keys, which refer you to grammatical points and page numbers for review.

5. Take Tests A, B, and C at the end of the book.
    Use the answer sheets provided.
    IMPORTANT: Be sure to time yourself or have a friend time you. Budget your time; work quickly but carefully.

6. Check your answers with the error keys that follow the tests.
    The error key will refer you to the grammatical point in question and the page number where it can be found.

7. Re-test if necessary.

VI

THE DIAGNOSTIC TEST

This diagnostic test will give you an idea of the kinds of grammatical points that will be tested in the *Structure and Written Expression* section of the TOEFL. After you have taken the diagnostic test, check your answers with the error key on page 18. The error key lists the correct answer for each question and tells where to find the review material for the grammatical point that is being tested. This diagnostic test will help identify the areas of English grammar that are most difficult for you. Then you can turn to the discussions of specific grammatical points and begin studying to review and improve your knowledge of standard written English.

Read the directions carefully before you start the diagnostic test. Circle the letter of the answer you choose.

DIAGNOSTIC TEST

Time allowed: 40 minutes

DIRECTIONS: Each of the following sentences contains four underlined words or phrases, marked A, B, C, and D. One of these words or phrases is *incorrect* in the sentence. Blacken the letter of the *incorrect* word or phrase on your answer sheet. Check your answers with the error key on page 18.

1. <u>Beautiful</u> is <u>in</u> the eye <u>of</u> the <u>beholder</u>.
     A   B   C   D

2. The baby showed a <u>noticeable</u> distaste <u>for</u> <u>these kind</u> of
                    A   B   C

   prepared <u>baby</u> food.
           D

3. They cannot go camping <u>right</u> now <u>because</u> they are
                       A   B

   <u>taking care of</u> a <u>three-weeks-old</u> baby.
        C   D

4. They went <u>into</u> the Superstition Mountains <u>in search for</u> the Lost
             A   B

   Dutchman's Mine and were <u>never</u> <u>heard from</u> again.
                            C   D

5. The young girl dreamed <u>a dream</u> <u>that</u> she <u>was being</u> carried
                          A   B   C

   away <u>by</u> monsters.
        D

6. If <u>it</u> <u>will rain</u> this afternoon, we <u>will have</u> to <u>cancel</u> the picnic.
      A   B   C   D

7. <u>Are</u> you familiar <u>of</u> the <u>latest</u> scientific developments <u>in</u> the field?
    A   B   C   D

8. Henry is the sort of <u>a</u> man <u>who</u> will give <u>you</u> the shirt <u>off</u>
                      A   B   C   D

   his back.

9. Give the package to <u>whomever</u> <u>has</u> the authority <u>to sign</u> for <u>it</u>.
                      A   B   C   D

10. When he <u>visited</u> the doctor, the doctor told <u>John</u> that he
            A   B

    <u>should gone</u> to the hospital <u>immediately</u>.
       C   D

11. Robert often <u>wishes</u> he <u>was</u> better prepared for his exams, but he
                 A   B

    will probably <u>never</u> change his <u>poor</u> study habits.
                C   D

12. This refrigerator is <u>very</u> old <u>to keep</u> things <u>at</u> a proper
                      A   B   C

    temperature.
       D

13. The meeting was so length that many people had to leave before
                 A   B   C

     it concluded.
     D

14. John was quick to inform us that his friend Vicky was most pop-
              A   B   C   D

     ular, intelligent girl in his class.

15. The director of the program advised the students to avoid to waste
                              A   B

     time reading material that was so out-of-date.
          C   D

16. There was not enough time to completely fill out the form before
                  A   B   C

     the bell rang.
          D

17. Margie and Mary must have ate some bad food in the restaurant
                  A   B

     because they were very ill shortly after they left.
            C   D

18. The children were surprised when the teacher had them to close
                  A   B   C

     their books unexpectedly.
                D

19. Do you think you could lend me good pair of gloves to wear to
                  A   B   C   D

     the wedding?

20. His speech was a careful worded attempt to evade his responsi-
                  A   B   D

     bility in the matter.
         D

21. The Joneses have visited Hawaii and Alaska, and they assure me
                  A   B

     that they like Alaska the best.
         C   D

22. We <u>must have</u> <u>a</u> exact count of the <u>number</u> of people expected
          A   B   C

to attend the <u>closing</u> ceremonies.
               D

23. The <u>stage</u> production that we <u>saw</u> in New York was very much
        A   B

as the one we <u>had previously seen</u> in London.
C   D

24. Did you hear <u>many</u> news about the <u>political</u> situation <u>while</u> you
             A   B   C

were <u>in</u> that country?
     D

25. <u>Both</u> John, Bob and Tom are <u>outstanding</u> golfers and <u>reasonably</u>
   A   B   C

<u>good</u> tennis players.
D

26. Kathy was definitely <u>a faster</u> swimmer <u>than</u> <u>anyone</u> on her team
                    A   B   C

and appeared <u>headed</u> for the state championship.
             D

27. The article suggests <u>that</u> when a person is under unusual stress
                  A

<u>you</u> should be <u>especially</u> careful to eat a <u>well-balanced</u> diet.
B   C   D

28. <u>Economics</u>, with <u>their</u> widespread range of practical application,
       A   B

<u>is</u> of great interest to government leaders <u>throughout</u> the world.
C   D

29. The Tyrrels had <u>such warm welcome</u> from their family that they
               A

were <u>overwhelmed</u> and <u>could not speak</u> for a <u>few</u> minutes.
      B   C   D

30. <u>Even though</u> he was exhausted, John wrote <u>to his parents</u> <u>a</u>
     A   B   C

letter <u>explaining</u> the situation.
      D

31. <u>Since</u> I have so <u>many</u> letters to write, I am going to buy several
   A   B

    boxes <u>of</u> <u>stationary</u>.
        C   D

32. Our friends <u>got</u> a <u>bank</u> loan <u>for to buy</u> <u>a</u> new car.
         A   B   C   D

33. By the time Robert <u>will finish</u> <u>writing</u> the first draft of his paper,
                A   B

    <u>most</u> of the other students will be completing <u>their</u> final draft.
    C   D

34. Some members <u>of</u> the committee were opposed <u>to use</u> the club
             A   B

    <u>members'</u> money to redecorate the <u>meeting</u> hall.
    C   D

35. I was very <u>shocked</u> to see <u>how much</u> my grandmother <u>she</u> had
            A   B   C

    aged <u>since</u> the last time we visited.
    D

36. Our supervisor finally noticed that it <u>was</u> <u>we</u>, <u>Diana and me</u>,
                              A B   C

    who always turned in our reports <u>on</u> time.
                            D

37. <u>In</u> our opinion that girl is <u>enough</u> beautiful <u>to be</u> a <u>movie</u> star.
    A   B   C   D

38. The report that Karl wrote <u>on</u> the mating behavior <u>of</u> the bees in
                      A   B

    this area was <u>definitely</u> better than <u>Bob</u>.
              C   D

39. We were pleased to have the opportunity to watch
    <u>such talented dancers</u> <u>to perform</u> <u>a</u> <u>highly</u> acclaimed new ballet.
           A   B   C D

40. The flag <u>is risen</u> at 6:30 <u>every</u> morning <u>without fail</u>.
          A   B   C   D

41. When the Claybornes bought their new home, they painted <u>every</u>
                                                              A

    room, <u>laid</u> carpet in the living room and hall, and <u>had refinished</u>
          B   C

    the <u>kitchen</u> cabinets.
        D

42. That student from Mexico <u>who</u> <u>is rooming</u> with Bill Smith reminds
                              A   B

    <u>me</u> <u>to</u> my uncle.
    C   D

43. When <u>they</u> travel to Europe, the Harrises like to stay in Paris and
         A

    <u>visiting</u> <u>as</u> <u>many</u> art galleries as possible.
    B   C   D

44. She <u>never is</u> <u>diligent</u> <u>about</u> <u>practicing</u> the piano.
        A   B   C   D

45. <u>During</u> that terrible snowstorm, the police <u>demanded</u> that people
    A   B

    <u>stayed off</u> Highway 101 <u>except</u> in cases of emergency.
    C   D

46. He <u>refused</u> <u>to tell</u> <u>us</u> why <u>was he</u> crying.
       A   B   C   D

47. Please <u>be</u> sure that everybody has <u>their</u> ticket ready <u>to give</u> to
           A   B   C

    the man <u>at</u> the door.
            D

48. We believe that he already feels very <u>badly</u> about his mistake
                                          A

    and we <u>have decided</u> to take <u>no</u> <u>further</u> action.
           B   C   D

49. <u>They</u> <u>who</u> are willing <u>to spend</u> the necessary time will find this
    A   B   C

    workshop to be a <u>rewarding</u> experience.
                     D

50. Please see <u>if</u> you can <u>repair</u> the <u>door's knob</u> <u>before</u> Saturday
         A   B   C   D

morning.

51. The passenger <u>only had</u> a five-dollar <u>bill</u> <u>with</u> him <u>when</u> he
              A   B C   D

boarded the bus.

52. It is <u>not longer</u> necessary <u>for</u> all employees
       A   B

<u>to wear an identification badge</u> <u>in order to work</u> in the vault.
           C   D

53. In <u>the</u> chapter one of that book there <u>is</u> a <u>really</u> good explana-
     A   B   C

tion of photosynthesis, <u>complete with</u> illustrations.
                     D

54. The salesman told me <u>that</u> a good set of tires <u>were supposed</u>
                 A   B

<u>to last</u> <u>at least</u> twenty thousand miles.
  C   D

55. <u>Sitting</u> under an umbrella at a tiny table in a sidewalk cafe, Bob
    A

was <u>startled</u> when a gust of wind <u>suddenly</u> carried <u>it</u> away.
      B   C   D

DIRECTIONS: For each of the following, select the letter of the one word or words that best complete(s) the sentence and write it (them) in the space provided at the left.

56. Riding my bicycle home from school, _____ as I went around the corner.

(A) a car hit me
(B) I was striked by a car
(C) I was struck by a car
(D) I was struck with a car

57. Doctor Martin is the kind of doctor _____ will take pains to be thorough.

   (A) which
   (B) who
   (C) whom
   (D) what

58. The two doctors received an award of several thousand dollars _____.

   (A) to be divided equally between them
   (B) which was supposed to be divided in an equal way between them
   (C) to be divided equally among them
   (D) which was to be divided between them in such a way that they would each receive an equal share

59. _____, he was able to answer all the questions on the examination.

   (A) Reading all the required material
   (B) Having reading all the required material
   (C) Having read all the required material
   (D) As it was the case that he had read all the required material

60. Exhausted, we went directly to bed and _____.

   (A) ignored him knocking on our door
   (B) ignored his knocking on our door
   (C) his knocking on our door was ignored by us
   (D) ignored his knocking with our door

61. John does not swim _____.

   (A) as fastly as Fred
   (B) as fast than Fred
   (C) as fast as Fred
   (D) as fast like Fred

62. Shakespeare wrote many plays, but in my opinion *The Merchant of Venice* was _____.

   (A) the better
   (B) the best
   (C) the goodest
   (D) the most good

63. _____ that the president's economic policy will help curb inflation.

    (A) The hope
    (B) It is hoped
    (C) Hoping
    (D) To hope

64. _____ your helpful suggestions, we are sending you a copy of our latest book.

    (A) In consideration of
    (B) For consideration of
    (C) With consideration for
    (D) In consideration with

65. John studied accounting _____ while he was at Yale.

    (A) and also pursued economics
    (B) and economics
    (C) and he also studied economics
    (D) and economics was also studied by him

Check your answers with the error key on page 18.

ERROR KEY

_A_ 1.   (*Beauty*). See *Parts of Speech*, page 193.

_C_ 2.   (*this* kind). See *Demonstratives*, page 34.

_D_ 3.   (three-*week*-old). See *Hyphenated or Compound Adjectives*, page 33.

_B_ 4.   (in search *of*). See *Prepositions in Combinations*, page 198.

_A_ 5.   (*dreamed that*). See *Wordiness*, page 162.

_B_ 6.   (If it *rains*). See *Conditionals*, page 82.

_B_ 7.   (familiar *with*). See *Prepositions in Combinations*, page 198.

_A_ 8.   (sort *of man*). See *Substandard*, page 166.

_A_ 9.   (to *whoever* has). See *Who/Whom*, page 111.

_C_ 10. (should *go*). See *Modals*, page 85.

_B_ 11. (*were* better prepared). See *Wishes*, page 80.

_A_ 12. (*too* old). See *Too*, *Very*, and *Enough*, page 52.

_A_ 13. (so *long* that). See *Cause and Result*, page 47.

_D_ 14. (*the* most popular). See *Superlatives*, page 44.

_B_ 15. (to avoid *wasting*). See *Verbals*, page 87.

_B_ 16. (*fill out completely*). See *Split Infinitives*, page 24.

_B_ 17. (must have *eaten*). See *Past Participles*, page 91.

_C_ 18. (had them *close*). See *Verbals*, page 87.

_B_ 19. (a good *pair*). See *Articles*, page 50.

_A_ 20. (*carefully worded*). See *Adjective/Adverb Confusion*, page 27.

_D_ 21. (Alaska *better*). See *Comparatives*, page 41.

_B_ 22. (*an* exact count). See *Articles*, page 50.

_C_ 23. (much *like* the one). See *Sameness and Similarity*, page 39.

_A_ 24. (*much* news). See *Few*, *Little*, *Much* and *Many*, page 35.

_A_ 25. (*John, Bob, and Tom*). See *Correlative Conjunctions*, page 187.

_C_ 26. (anyone *else*). See *Comparatives*, page 41.

_B_ 27. (*he* should be). See *Person*, page 117.

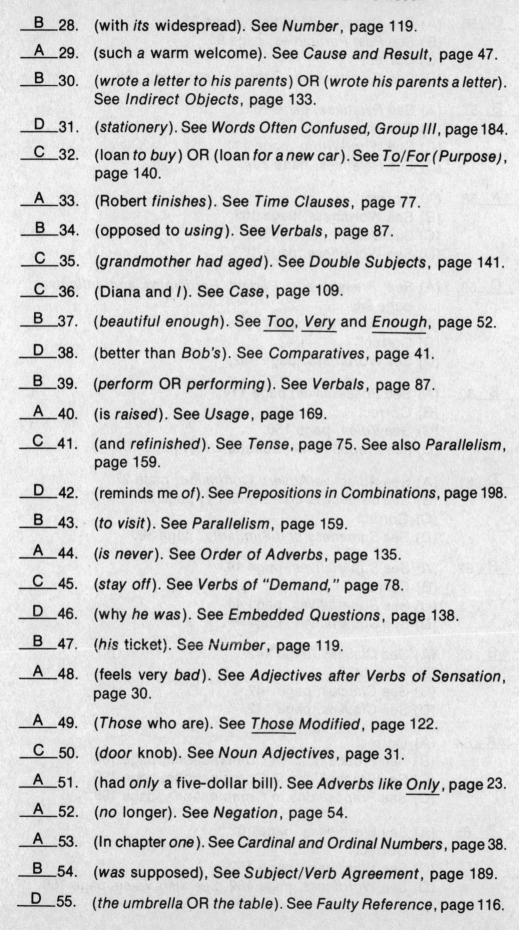

__B__ 28. (with *its* widespread). See *Number*, page 119.

__A__ 29. (such *a* warm welcome). See *Cause and Result*, page 47.

__B__ 30. (*wrote a letter to his parents*) OR (*wrote his parents a letter*). See *Indirect Objects*, page 133.

__D__ 31. (*stationery*). See *Words Often Confused, Group III*, page 184.

__C__ 32. (loan *to buy*) OR (loan *for a new car*). See *To/For (Purpose)*, page 140.

__A__ 33. (Robert *finishes*). See *Time Clauses*, page 77.

__B__ 34. (opposed to *using*). See *Verbals*, page 87.

__C__ 35. (*grandmother had aged*). See *Double Subjects*, page 141.

__C__ 36. (Diana and *I*). See *Case*, page 109.

__B__ 37. (*beautiful enough*). See *Too, Very* and *Enough*, page 52.

__D__ 38. (better than *Bob's*). See *Comparatives*, page 41.

__B__ 39. (*perform* OR *performing*). See *Verbals*, page 87.

__A__ 40. (is *raised*). See *Usage*, page 169.

__C__ 41. (and *refinished*). See *Tense*, page 75. See also *Parallelism*, page 159.

__D__ 42. (reminds me *of*). See *Prepositions in Combinations*, page 198.

__B__ 43. (*to visit*). See *Parallelism*, page 159.

__A__ 44. (*is never*). See *Order of Adverbs*, page 135.

__C__ 45. (*stay off*). See *Verbs of "Demand,"* page 78.

__D__ 46. (why *he was*). See *Embedded Questions*, page 138.

__B__ 47. (*his* ticket). See *Number*, page 119.

__A__ 48. (feels very *bad*). See *Adjectives after Verbs of Sensation*, page 30.

__A__ 49. (*Those* who are). See *Those Modified*, page 122.

__C__ 50. (*door* knob). See *Noun Adjectives*, page 31.

__A__ 51. (had *only* a five-dollar bill). See *Adverbs like Only*, page 23.

__A__ 52. (*no* longer). See *Negation*, page 54.

__A__ 53. (In chapter *one*). See *Cardinal and Ordinal Numbers*, page 38.

__B__ 54. (*was* supposed), See *Subject/Verb Agreement*, page 189.

__D__ 55. (*the umbrella* OR *the table*). See *Faulty Reference*, page 116.

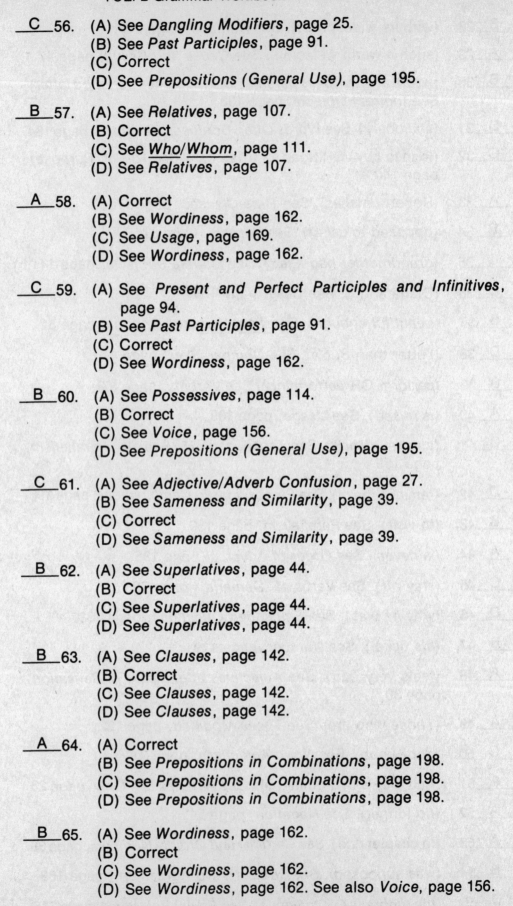

__C__ 56. (A) See *Dangling Modifiers*, page 25.
           (B) See *Past Participles*, page 91.
           (C) Correct
           (D) See *Prepositions (General Use)*, page 195.

__B__ 57. (A) See *Relatives*, page 107.
           (B) Correct
           (C) See *Who/Whom*, page 111.
           (D) See *Relatives*, page 107.

__A__ 58. (A) Correct
           (B) See *Wordiness*, page 162.
           (C) See *Usage*, page 169.
           (D) See *Wordiness*, page 162.

__C__ 59. (A) See *Present and Perfect Participles and Infinitives*,
               page 94.
           (B) See *Past Participles*, page 91.
           (C) Correct
           (D) See *Wordiness*, page 162.

__B__ 60. (A) See *Possessives*, page 114.
           (B) Correct
           (C) See *Voice*, page 156.
           (D) See *Prepositions (General Use)*, page 195.

__C__ 61. (A) See *Adjective/Adverb Confusion*, page 27.
           (B) See *Sameness and Similarity*, page 39.
           (C) Correct
           (D) See *Sameness and Similarity*, page 39.

__B__ 62. (A) See *Superlatives*, page 44.
           (B) Correct
           (C) See *Superlatives*, page 44.
           (D) See *Superlatives*, page 44.

__B__ 63. (A) See *Clauses*, page 142.
           (B) Correct
           (C) See *Clauses*, page 142.
           (D) See *Clauses*, page 142.

__A__ 64. (A) Correct
           (B) See *Prepositions in Combinations*, page 198.
           (C) See *Prepositions in Combinations*, page 198.
           (D) See *Prepositions in Combinations*, page 198.

__B__ 65. (A) See *Wordiness*, page 162.
           (B) Correct
           (C) See *Wordiness*, page 162.
           (D) See *Wordiness*, page 162. See also *Voice*, page 156.

VII

ABBREVIATIONS

This is a list of the abbreviations used in the review sections of this book.

adj.	adjective
adv.	adverb
aux.	auxiliary
cl.	clause
CN	count noun
comp.	comparative
conj.	conjunction
d.o.	direct object
fut.	future
infin. (or *to* + V)	infinitive
i.o.	indirect object
irr.	irregular
N	noun
NCN	non-count noun
neg.	negative
obj.	object

part.	participle
past part.	past participle
past perf.	past perfect
perf. part.	perfect participle
pl.	plural
prep.	preposition
pres.	present
pron.	pronoun
QW	question word
S	subject
sing.	singular
suprl.	superlative
to+*have*+past part.	perfect infinitive
to+V (or infin.)	infinitive
V	simple form of the verb
V+*ing*	present participle or gerund

VIII

MODIFIERS

MODIFIERS—ADVERBS LIKE *ONLY*

Adverbs like *only* come as close as possible to the adjectives, verbs, or other adverbs they modify.

ADV. ADJ.
She has *only three* dollars.

ADV. VERB
He *only saw* her; he did not speak to her.

ADV. ADV.
Only downstairs can one find a real bargain.

NOTE:

Other adverbs like *only* are: *just*, *nearly*, *hardly*, *almost*, and *scarcely*.

ERROR EXAMPLES

A. WRONG: We only have four hours to finish this paper.
   RIGHT: We have *only* four hours to finish this paper.

B. WRONG: She just wants to take one class.
   RIGHT: She wants to take *just* one class.

C. WRONG: That house nearly costs sixty thousand dollars.
   RIGHT: That house costs *nearly* sixty thousand dollars.

D. WRONG: She was so quiet that hardly he noticed her.
   RIGHT: She was so quiet that he *hardly* noticed her.

E. WRONG: They almost drove six hundred miles.
    RIGHT: They drove *almost* six hundred miles.

EXERCISE: Put "C" if the sentence is correct. Put "X" if the adverb is not as close as possible to the word it modifies.

_____1.   If you go to window five, you will have to wait only five minutes.

_____2.   You can use these machines only between 9 A.M. and 5 P.M.

_____3.   He hardly knows any English.

_____4.   That shirt almost cost twenty dollars.

_____5.   Just ten people will be able to go today.

_____6.   You hardly have enough time to do the first exercise.

_____7.   We had to wait nearly ten minutes for the movie to begin.

_____8.   She scarcely slept five hours last night.

_____9.   We want to borrow only ten dollars.

_____10. The soldiers only killed one person during the battle.

Check your answers with the error key on page 63.

MODIFIERS—SPLIT INFINITIVES

The *infinitive* is *to* + the simple form of the verb (*V*). Do not put an adverb between *to* and *V*.

TO + V   ADV.
He refused *to fill out* the form *completely*.

TO + V   ADV.
They have decided *to repeat* the directions *carefully*.

TO + V   ADV.
We hope *to inform* him *quickly*.

ERROR EXAMPLES

A. WRONG: He wanted to carefully read the directions.
    RIGHT: He wanted *to read* the directions *carefully*.

B. WRONG: To thoroughly understand the subject, ask an expert.
    RIGHT: *To understand* the subject *thoroughly*, ask an expert.

C. WRONG: He was looking for a way to rapidly complete the job.
    RIGHT: He was looking for a way *to complete* the job *rapidly*.

EXERCISE: Put "C" if the sentence is correct. Put "X" if any word comes between *to* and the simple form of the verb.

_____1. We decided to leave the area quickly.

_____2. He seemed to easily understand the situation.

_____3. To really make him happy would be impossible.

_____4. She used a scale to accurately weigh the vegetables.

_____5. Do not try to completely finish your homework before dinner.

_____6. To hastily read the material is not enough for good comprehension.

_____7. He began to chatter about the event excitedly.

_____8. Please try to entirely revise your work before you leave.

_____9. The teacher wanted to know positively whether or not the students could come to the picnic.

_____10. Bob is going to soon decide on his future course of study.

Check your answers with the error key on page 63.

MODIFIERS—DANGLING MODIFIERS

The subject of the main clause must be the same as the understood subject of the introductory phrase. In other words, the introductory phrase modifies the subject of the main clause.

INTRODUCTORY PHRASE   MAIN CLAUSE
Looking at his watch , <u>Mr. Jones</u> *got up and left.*
                SUBJECT

Who looked at his watch?   *Mr. Jones*

Who got up and left?   *Mr. Jones*

INTRODUCTORY PHRASE   MAIN CLAUSE
Compared to his father , <u>John</u> *is a tall man.*
              SUBJECT

Who is compared to his father?   *John*

Who is a tall man?   *John*

INTRODUCTORY PHRASE   MAIN CLAUSE
To make a collect phone call , <u>Mary</u> *must speak to the operator.*
              SUBJECT

Who is making a collect phone call?   *Mary*

Who must speak to the operator?   *Mary*

INTRODUCTORY PHRASE   MAIN CLAUSE
While a dancer in New York , <u>Kathy</u> *injured her leg.*
              SUBJECT

Who was a dancer in New York?   *Kathy*

Who injured her leg?   *Kathy*

ERROR EXAMPLES

A.   WRONG: Running home from school, a dog bit me.
      RIGHT: *Running home from school, I was bitten by a dog.*

B.   WRONG: When only a child, my father took me to the circus.
      RIGHT: *When only a child, I was taken to the circus by my father.*

C.   WRONG: Hidden in his pocket, George left the room with the key.
      RIGHT: *Having hidden the key in his pocket, George left the room.*

D.   WRONG: To understand the directions, they must be read carefully.
      RIGHT: *To understand the directions, one must read them carefully.*

EXERCISE: Put "C" if the sentence is correct. Put "X" if there is a dangling-modifier error.

_____1. Playing in the street, the truck hit the child.

_____2. By painting and repairing as needed, your home can be kept in good condition.

_____3. Before leaving, Jane kissed me goodbye.

_____4. Addressed and stamped, I dropped the letter in the slot.

_____5. While a student at college, my mother met my father.

_____6. Walking toward the church, the stained-glass windows looked beautiful.

_____7. To understand the subject, a great deal of studying must be done.

_____8. Skiing down the steep hill, my heart beat crazily.

_____9. Watching her daughter play, Mary thought about life as a mother.

_____10. Once learned, a language cannot easily be forgotten.

_____11. When only a child, my father taught me how to play soccer.

_____12. Studying and reading, the day passed quickly.

_____13. To make a good cup of coffee, one must begin with high-quality coffee beans.

_____14. Sitting alone in his room, the strange noise frightened him.

_____15. Wrapped in pretty green paper, Phyllis put the package on the table.

Check your answers with the error key on page 64.

MODIFIERS—ADJECTIVE/ADVERB CONFUSION

1. *Adjectives* modify nouns (N) and pronouns.

ADJ.   N   ADJ.   N
His *recent accident* caused a *sudden change* in his behavior.

PRON.   ADJ.
He is *intelligent*.

2. *Adverbs* modify verbs (V).

VERB   ADV.   VERB
He *had* an accident *recently*, and his behavior *changed*

ADV.
suddenly.

VERB   ADV.
He *spoke intelligently*.

3. Adverbs also modify adjectives.

ADV.   ADJ.
He grew an *especially small* tree.

ADV.   ADJ.
He was a *highly motivated* young man.

ADV.   ADJ.
It was a *cleverly planned* operation.

4. Adverbs also modify other adverbs.

ADV.   ADV.
She could run *very quickly*.

NOTES:

a. Most adverbs end in *-ly*.

b. Some words have the same form for the adjective and adverb:

Adjective	*Adverb*
late	late
fast	fast
hard	hard

(Do not add *-ly* to these words.)

c. The adverb for the adjective *good* is *well*.

ERROR EXAMPLES

A. WRONG: Do it carefully, if not perfect.
    RIGHT: Do it carefully, if not *perfectly*.

B. WRONG: He is an extreme pleasant person.
    RIGHT: He is an *extremely* pleasant person.

C. WRONG: It was an interesting designed museum.
    RIGHT: It was an *interestingly* designed museum.

D. WRONG: He worked hardly at the factory all day.
    RIGHT: He worked *hard* at the factory all day.

E. WRONG: You should order that book real soon.
    RIGHT: You should order that book *really* soon.

F. WRONG: My sister plays the piano very good.
    RIGHT: My sister plays the piano very *well*.

EXERCISE: Put "C" if the sentence is correct. Put "X" if there is an adjective or adverb error.

_____1.   The bus arrived lately, so I missed my first class.

_____2.   We did not pass the test, but we certainly tried hard.

_____3.   The train left at exactly 5:00 P.M.

_____4.   When Ms. Smith went to Germany, she bought an exquisitely carved vase.

_____5.   They had a real good chance of winning the national competition.

_____6.   Computers process data efficiently.

_____7.   We worked hard and saved enough money to take a trip.

_____8.   There was a hasty called meeting to discuss the bus strike.

_____9.   He was thorough interested in the subject.

_____10. That dress fits her perfectly.

_____11. She likes her students to arrive prompt for class.

_____12. We studied really hard for the test.

_____13. He was bright and attractive.

_____14. The child ran fastly to get to school.

_____15. He wrote his paper really good.

_____16. The careful organized tour of the city was a huge success.

_____17. You cannot possibly imagine how embarrassed I was yesterday.

_____18. Although he plays soccer well, he plays tennis bad.

_____19. I read an interestingly written report.

_____20. The time went by very fastly on our vacation.

Check your answers with the error key on page 64.

MODIFIERS—ADJECTIVES AFTER VERBS OF SENSATION

These verbs of sensation are generally followed by _adjectives*_, not by adverbs: _feel_, _look_, _seem_, _appear_, _taste_, _smell_, and _sound_.

VERB   ADJ.
He _feels bad_ .

VERB   ADJ.
The soup _smells delicious_ .

VERB   ADJ.
She _looked nervous_ before the test.

*These are also called "predicate adjectives."

ERROR EXAMPLES

A.   WRONG: Those flowers smell sweetly.
      RIGHT: Those flowers smell _sweet_.

B.   WRONG: That loud music sounds badly to me.
      RIGHT: That loud music sounds _bad_ to me.

C.   WRONG: He looks handsomely in black.
      RIGHT: He looks _handsome_ in black.

EXERCISE: Put "C" if the sentence is correct. Put "X" if there is an adjective or adverb error.

_____1. I felt sadly when I read the letter.

_____2. That gossip sounds malicious.

_____3. The wine tastes awfully, like vinegar.

_____4. The girls look adorable in their party costumes.

_____5. Our neighbor's music sounded loudly last night.

_____6. Laurie seemed quiet after she read her friend's letter.

_____7. The roses and lilacs smell nicely every spring.

_____8. Do not drink that milk; it tastes sourly.

_____9. My sister has always looked heavy because she has broad shoulders.

_____10. He appeared nervously as he began to take the exam.

Check your answers with the error key on page 65.

MODIFIERS—NOUN ADJECTIVES

The first noun (N) in the following pattern is used as an adjective.

N   N
You are all *language students* .

NOTES:

  a. When nouns are used as adjectives, they do *not* have plural or possessive forms.

  b. EXCEPTIONS: The following nouns always end in *-s* but are singular in number when they are used as names of courses or sciences: *physics*, *mathematics*, *economics*.

N   N
He is an *economics teacher* .

  BUT:

ADJ.   N
The current *economic situation* is extremely uncertain.

ERROR EXAMPLES

A.   WRONG: He is taking some histories classes this semester.
       RIGHT: He is taking some *history* classes this semester.

B.   WRONG: John turned in his term's paper this morning.
       RIGHT: John turned in his *term* paper this morning.

C.   WRONG: My friend is an economic major.
       RIGHT: My friend is an *economics* major.

EXERCISE: Put "C" if the sentence is correct. Put "X" if there is an error in the noun adjective.

_____1.   Tom drove past the police's station on his way to work.

_____2.   Joan Sutherland is my favorite opera singer.

_____3.   I need to have my car's license renewed.

_____4.   During the power shortage, the streets lights went out.

_____5.   He wanted to take an economic class.

_____6.   Many people are worried about the current world's situation.

_____7.   The news reporter was at the scene of the accident.

_____8.   Phyllis and Julie put up the party decorations.

_____9.   Three footballs teams were tied for first place.

_____10.   Mike is the new mathematics professor.

_____11.   We need some paper napkins for the picnic.

_____12.   The students did not like the dormitory's rules.

_____13.   The marble floor felt like ice.

_____14.   The television's repairman picked up my television set this morning.

_____15.   I went to three dances recitals last year.

_____16.   John bought some leather gloves yesterday.

_____17.   I need to buy a plane's ticket.

_____18.   He took many languages courses when he was in New York.

_____19.   She put a new table lamp in her living room.

_____20.   He is taking an advanced physic course this semester.

Check your answers with the error key on page 66.

MODIFIERS—HYPHENATED OR COMPOUND ADJECTIVES

Nouns (N) are sometimes found as part of *hyphenated* or *compound* adjectives (adjectives of more than one word joined by hyphens). These nouns are *never* plural.

HYPHENATED ADJ.
I bought a *four-hundred-year-old* painting in
Hong Kong.   N

HYPHENATED ADJ.
The president gave a *ten-minute* speech.
                              N

ERROR EXAMPLES

A. WRONG: I lived in a two-hundred-years-old house in Rome.
   RIGHT: I lived in a two-hundred-*year*-old house in Rome.

B. WRONG: He bought a three-hundred-dollars suit.
   RIGHT: He bought a three-hundred-*dollar* suit.

C. WRONG: The teacher told us to read the five-hundred-pages book.
   RIGHT: The teacher told us to read the five-hundred-*page* book.

D. WRONG: I have four fifty-minutes classes every day.
   RIGHT: I have four fifty-*minute* classes every day.

E. WRONG: She has just bought a new four-doors Ford.
   RIGHT: She has just bought a new four-*door* Ford.

EXERCISE: Put "C" if the sentence is correct. Put "X" if there is an error with a hyphenated adjective.

_____1. We signed up for a three-hour lab.

_____2. The police suspected a thirty-years-old man.

_____3. My mother bought some five-dollars-a-pound cheese.

_____4. John got a ten-speed bicycle for his birthday.

_____5. I visited the five-thousand-years-old pyramids in Egypt last summer.

_____6. John and Sue brought me a two-ounces bottle of French perfume.

_____7. My parents are going on a four-week European tour next month.

_____8. Most ten-month-old babies cannot walk.

_____9. They are studying the five-hundred-pages manual.

_____10. The Smiths have just purchased a ten-rooms house.

Check your answers with the error key on page 66.

MODIFIERS—DEMONSTRATIVES

The demonstratives *this* and *that* (singular) and *these* and *those* (plural) must agree in number with the nouns they modify.

SING. SING.
John does not like *this kind* of class.

PL.   PL.
What do you think of *these kinds* of chairs?

ERROR EXAMPLES

A. WRONG: These type of potato is native to Peru.
    RIGHT: *This* type of potato is native to Peru.

B. WRONG: That kinds of women are likely to succeed in business.
    RIGHT: *Those* kinds of women are likely to succeed in business.

C. WRONG: Jane never buys these brand of canned goods.
    RIGHT: Jane never buys *this* brand of canned goods.

EXERCISE: Put "C" if the sentence is correct. Put "X" if there is an error with the demonstrative modifiers.

_____1. They did not like those kinds of imported cars.

_____2. The farmers could not find any buyers for these class of wheat.

_____3. This kind of story is not suitable for young children.

_____4. Those kinds of books are fascinating and helpful.

_____5. Do you think we should buy these kind of flowers for the front yard?

_____6. Mary never shops in those kind of expensive specialty shops.

_____7. He took that news badly.

_____8. Bob should not have bought these pair of shoes.

_____9. This movies are restricted to people over 17 years of age.

_____10. Although Bill has owned many kinds of cars, he has never considered buying this kind before.

Check your answers with the error key on page 67.

MODIFIERS—*FEW, LITTLE, MUCH, AND MANY*

1. *Few*, *fewer*, and *fewest*, as well as *many*, are followed by *plural count nouns*.

PL. CN
There are *few students* from Japan in our English class.

PL. CN
This year we received *fewer replies* to our ad than ever before.

PL. CN
John has *the fewest chapters* left to read of anyone in the class.

PL. CN
There are *many reasons* to study hard for that test.

2. *Little*, *less*, and *least*, as well as *much*, are followed by *non-count nouns*.

NCN
He gave me a *little advice* about choosing a school.

NCN
Susan has *less money* than I.

NCN
He did *the least amount* of work of anyone in the class.

NCN
There is not *much time* to finish this job completely.

NOTES:

    a. In general, *plural count nouns* can be recognized by the *-s* plural form. However, do not forget that the following words are plural: *people*, *men*, *women*, *children*, and *police*.

    b. The following are examples of *non-count nouns: fruit*, *homework*, *bread*, *money*, *furniture*, and *time*. Do not add *-s* to these words.

    c. The word *news* looks plural, but it is a non-count noun. Example: Little *news* is coming from that country.

    d. For *number* and *amount* see *Style—Usage*, page 169.

================================

ERROR EXAMPLES

A. **WRONG:** There are much books on the shelf.
    RIGHT: There are *many* books on the shelf.

B. **WRONG:** There is not many industry in that town.
    RIGHT: There is not *much* industry in that town.

C. **WRONG:** He had few winter clothing when he arrived.
    RIGHT: He had *little* winter clothing when he arrived.

D. **WRONG:** You need a little dollars to buy this book.
    RIGHT: You need a *few* dollars to buy this book.

E. **WRONG:** Lloyd scored the least points in the basketball game.
    RIGHT: Lloyd scored the *fewest* points in the basketball game.

F. WRONG: Isabelle bought less than ten items.
    RIGHT: Isabelle bought *fewer* than ten items.

EXERCISE: Put "C" if the sentence is correct. Put "X" if there is an error with *many*, *few*, *much*, or *little*.

_____1. I do not like many sugar in my coffee.

_____2. They did not put much furniture in their new office.

_____3. We did not have much knowledge about physics.

_____4. Of the four people injured in the accident, the child needed the fewest medical attention.

_____5. John had so few news from his parents that he was worried.

_____6. I usually have little money at the end of the month.

_____7. Debby spent less time studying for the exam than Robin did.

_____8. He predicted that few people would die of radiation poisoning.

_____9. Bill has the least·cavities of anyone in his class.

_____10. We wanted to go on vacation, but we had few money.

_____11. There were so few good seats left that we decided not to buy tickets to the concert.

_____12. Nowadays much women are becoming lawyers.

_____13. That party did not have much entertainment.

_____14. There is not many news available on that subject.

_____15. During the war our government received fewer information about the situation in that country.

_____16. There were a little people waiting to buy tickets.

_____17. He had so many homework that he could not go to the movies.

_____18. Although she was rich, she wore little jewelry.

_____19. There were so much campus police at the football game that there was no trouble.

_____20. He did not eat many fruit in the winter.

Check your answers with the error key on page 67.

MODIFIERS—CARDINAL AND ORDINAL NUMBERS

There are two kinds of numbers, *cardinal* and *ordinal*.

Examples:

Cardinal	Ordinal
one	first
two	second
three	third
four	fourth
five	fifth
six	sixth
ten	tenth
twenty-one	twenty-first

The following two patterns are used to designate items in a series:

1. Ordinal numbers are used in this pattern: *the* + ordinal + noun (N)

   THE + ORDINAL + N
   The first book of the series is about verbs.

2. Cardinal numbers are used in this pattern: noun (N) + cardinal

   N + CARDINAL
   Book One of the series is about verbs.

NOTES:

a. Use *the* with ordinal numbers.

b. Do not use *the* with cardinal numbers.

c. Be careful to use the correct word order for each pattern.

ERROR EXAMPLES

A. WRONG: We are supposed to read the chapter seven for homework.

   RIGHT: We are supposed to read *chapter seven* for homework.

B. WRONG: Pick up your boarding passes at gate the fifth.
    RIGHT: Pick up your boarding passes at *gate five*.

C. WRONG: Terminal first on your right is Pan American.
    RIGHT: *The first terminal* on your right is Pan American.

D. WRONG: We reviewed lesson the tenth in class today.
    RIGHT: We reviewed lesson *ten* in class today.

E. WRONG: The subway stop second is Broadway.
    RIGHT: *The second* subway stop is Broadway.

EXERCISE: Put "C" if the sentence is correct. Put "X" if there is a number error.

_____1. The first checkout stand is for cash-customers only.

_____2. The answer is in the line fifteen on page four.

_____3. Do the exercise one in your book.

_____4. Pick up your receipt at teller fourth.

_____5. The car designers modified their plans for the hundredth time.

_____6. Pick up your check at window the third.

_____7. I met him on the second day of the fall semester.

_____8. You will find the bread in aisle the first.

_____9. The well-known basketball player from Chicago made the first points of the game.

_____10. The instructions are on the six page.

Check your answers with the error key on page 68.

MODIFIERS—SAMENESS AND SIMILARITY

Sameness and similarity are expressed by the following patterns:

1. *like* or *the same as*

    Your car is *like* mine. (*similarity*)

    Your car is *the same as* mine. (*sameness*)

2. *the same* + noun + *as*

                        N
    John is *the same height as* Bill.

                       N
    Mary is *the same age as* Valerie.

3. *as* + adjective + *as*

                ADJ.
    John is *as tall as* Bill.

                ADJ.
    Mary is *as old as* Valerie.

ERROR EXAMPLES

A. WRONG: I would like to have an apartment as the one my friend has.
    RIGHT: I would like to have an apartment *like* the one my friend has.

B. WRONG: Their backyard is as beautiful like a picture.
    RIGHT: Their backyard is *as beautiful as* a picture.

C. WRONG: He looks as his grandmother.
    RIGHT: He looks *like* his grandmother.

D. WRONG: This book is the same long as that one.
    RIGHT: This book is *as long as* that one.

E. WRONG: John is as tall than Bob.
    RIGHT: John is *as tall as* Bob.

F. WRONG: Mike's eyes are the same color that mine.
    RIGHT: Mike's eyes are *the same color as* mine.

G. WRONG: Her job pays the same salary like mine.
    RIGHT: Her job pays *the same salary as* mine.

EXERCISE: Put a "C" if the sentence is correct. Put an "X" if the comparative pattern is incorrect.

_____1. I would like to go to a school as the one my sister goes to.

_____2. His hair is the same length as mine.

_____3. Your apartment is the same size to mine.

_____4. That garden is as beautiful like the one in the park.

_____5. Elizabeth is the same weight as her girlfriend.

_____6. Your homework is the same as mine.

_____7. She looks as her mother.

_____8. This blouse is the same expensive as that one.

_____9. I would like to buy some earrings like yours.

_____10. He is as intelligent than his brother.

_____11. Your sofa is almost like hers.

_____12. He looks like his grandfather.

_____13. Tom's suit is the same style that Bob's.

_____14. This material feels like silk.

_____15. Your shoes are the same color like mine.

Check your answers with the error key on page 69.

MODIFIERS—COMPARATIVES

1. One-syllable adjectives and two-syllable adjectives ending in -y*
   form the comparative by adding -er.

   ADJ.   ADJ. + -ER
   John is *tall*, but Bill is *taller*.

   ADJ.   ADJ. + -ER
   Mr. Smith is *busy*, but Mr. Brown is *busier*.

   *Change the -y to -i before adding -er.

2. Most two- and three-syllable adjectives form the comparative by putting *more* before the adjective.

ADJ.   MORE + ADJ.

Betty is *beautiful*, but her sister is *more beautiful*.

3. Some adjectives have irregular comparatives and must be memorized. Examples: *good*, *better*; *bad*, *worse*.

ADJ.   IRR. COMP.

This book is *good*, but that one is *better.*

ADJ.   IRR. COMP.

This soup is *bad*, but that soup is *worse.*

4. *Than* is the *only* structure word that can follow comparatives.

COMP. + THAN

Their problem is *worse than* your problem.

NOTES:

  a. Do not use both *-er* and *more* in the same comparative structure.

  b. Be careful to use only *than* after a comparative structure.

  c. Be careful to use the comparative for two items, not three or more. For three or more, use the *superlative*. See *Modifiers—Superlatives*, page 44.

ERROR EXAMPLES

There are two main kinds of errors with comparatives, errors in structure and errors in logic.

Structure Errors:

A. WRONG: Betty is more smarter than her classmates.
    RIGHT: Betty is *smarter* than her classmates.

B. WRONG: This building is more expensive as that one.
    RIGHT: This building is more expensive *than* that one.

C. WRONG: Jane had much longer hair that her sister.
    RIGHT: Jane had much longer hair *than* her sister.

D. WRONG: I own two cars, a Ford and a Chevrolet. I like the Chevrolet the best.

    RIGHT: I own two cars, a Ford and a Chevrolet. I like the Chevrolet *better*.

Logic Errors:

1. Do not compare two nouns that cannot be compared.

E. WRONG: John's salary was much larger than Bob.
            (*Salary* cannot be compared to *Bob*.)
    RIGHT: John's salary was much larger than *that of Bob.*

OR

John's salary was much larger than *Bob's.*

F. WRONG: The number of people at the meeting is larger than last week.
            (*Number* cannot be compared to *week*.)
    RIGHT: The number of people at the meeting is larger than *that at last week's meeting.*

2. Do not compare a noun to itself.

G. WRONG: Mary is smarter than anybody in her class.
            (Mary is a member of the class. Mary cannot be smarter than herself.)
    RIGHT: Mary is smarter than *any other student* in the class.

OR

Mary is smarter than *anybody else* in the class.

H. WRONG: Alaska is larger than any state in the United States.
            (Alaska is one of the states in the United States. It cannot be larger than itself.)
    RIGHT: Alaska is larger than *any other state* in the United States.

EXERCISE: Put "C" if the sentence is correct. Put "X" if there is an error in the comparative pattern.

_____1. This book is more better than that one.

_____2. This year's prices will certainly be much higher as last year's prices.

_____ 3. Since there were two possible ways to get to New York, we had to decide which one was better.

_____ 4. The customs in his country are more traditional than those in the United States.

_____ 5. Her letter was more friendlier than his.

_____ 6. She was happier than anybody in her family.

_____ 7. Nancy was luckier than Fred in Las Vegas.

_____ 8. Betty's homework is usually more organized than that of any other student's in the class.

_____ 9 The weather was much hotter this year than 1970.

_____ 10. The final exam was more difficult than the mid-semester exam.

_____ 11. The first performance was more crowded as the second one.

_____ 12. The new student reads faster than anyone else in the class.

_____ 13. Fred's project proposal was much more economical than Brad's.

_____ 14. Robert's new home is more expensive than any house in the neighborhood.

_____ 15. Henry had a rather bad accident, and it was a miracle that he was not hurt more worse than he was.

Check your answers with the error key on page 69.

MODIFIERS—SUPERLATIVES

Use the *superlative* to make a comparison among three or more things.

1. One-syllable adjectives and two-syllable adjectives ending in *-y* form the superlative by adding *-est*. Always use *the* in the superlative pattern.

THE + ADJ. + -EST
Bill is taller than John, but Bob is *the tallest*.

THE + ADJ. + -EST
Bill is happier than John, but Bob is *the happiest*.

2. Two- and three-syllable adjectives form the superlative by putting *the most* before the adjective.

Susan is more beautiful than Betty, but Jane is

THE MOST + ADJ.
the most beautiful.

3. Some adjectives have irregular superlatives that must be memorized. For example: *good*, *the best*; *bad*, *the worst*.

Your book is better than his book, but our book is

THE + IRR. SUPRL.
the best.

Your problem is worse than mine, but his problem is

THE + IRR. SUPRL.
the worst.

NOTES:

a. Always use *the* in the superlative pattern.

b. Be careful not to use *-est* and *most* in the same superlative pattern.

c. Do not put *than* after the superlative.

d. Be careful to use the superlative for three or more items. Use the comparative for two items. See *Modifiers—Comparatives*, page 41.

ERROR EXAMPLES

A. WRONG: Yesterday was coldest day of the year.
   RIGHT: Yesterday was *the* coldest day of the year.

B. WRONG: John is the smartest student than anyone else in the class.
   RIGHT: John is the smartest student *in the class*.

C. WRONG: We went to Ann's Restaurant, Ted's Diner, and Tom's Cafe, and Ann's Restaurant served better food.
   RIGHT: We went to Ann's Restaurant, Ted's Diner, and Tom's Cafe, and Ann's Restaurant served *the best* food.

D. WRONG: I took mathematics, French, and history last semester, and the mathematics course was the better.
    RIGHT: I took mathematics, French, and history last semester, and the mathematics course was *the best*.

E. WRONG: She was the most beautifulest woman I had ever seen.
    RIGHT: She was the *most beautiful* woman I had ever seen.

EXERCISE: Put "C" if the sentence is correct. Put "X" if there is an error in the superlative pattern.

_____1. They were the most poorest people I had ever seen.

_____2. West Germany is one of the most highly industrialized nations in the world.

_____3. When he won the contest, he was the most surprised person than the other contestants.

_____4. I went to Belgium, Holland, and England last year, and I liked Belgium better.

_____5. Is the Sahara the largest desert in the world?

_____6. August is hottest and most humid month of the year.

_____7. It was the most biggest building I had ever seen.

_____8. That company sold the most sophisticated computer equipment that we had ever found.

_____9. Dr. Henderson was the most thorough doctor than Jane had ever known.

_____10. John, Phyllis, and Mary were all saving money to go to Egypt, and John saved the most.

_____11. Paula, Susie, and Jill bought new homes, but Paula's was more elegant.

_____12. Peking is most densely populated city in the world.

_____13. The damage caused by the hurricane was the worst than had ever occurred in that state.

_____14. She bought a new color television, a stereo unit, and an AM/FM radio, and the television was the most expensive.

_____15. Mary is the fastest runner than the other team members.

_____16. You can use any of these three pens, but the red one is the best for marking on heavy material.

_____17. That place serves the goodest ice cream in town.

_____18. Dr. Jones was certainly among the smartest men I had ever known.

_____19. He got the baddest grade he had ever received on an exam.

_____20. The crimes committed by that murderer were the most heinous in the history of that town.

Check your answers with the error key on page 70.

MODIFIERS—CAUSE AND RESULT

Cause-and-result clauses are expressed by the following patterns:

1. *so*

a) *so* + adjective + *that*

ADJ.
He was *so tired that* he fell asleep.

b) *so* + adverb + *that*

ADV.
He reads *so slowly that* he can never finish his homework.

*c) *so* + $\begin{matrix} many \\ few \end{matrix}$ + count noun + *that*

CN
She had *so many problems that* she could not concentrate.

CN
There were *so few tickets* sold *that* the concert was cancelled.

*d) *so* + $\begin{matrix} much \\ little \end{matrix}$ + non-count noun + *that*

NCN

The storm caused *so much damage that* the people were forced to leave their homes.

NCN

They had *so little interest* in the project *that* it failed.

2. *such*

   a) *such* + adjective + plural count noun + *that*

   ADJ.   PL. CN

   They were *such good students that* they passed the TOEFL.

   b) *such* + adjective + non-count noun + *that*

   ADJ.   NCN

   It was *such good cake that* we asked for more.

3. *so* or *such* (singular count nouns can use either of the following patterns)

   a) *so* + adjective + *a* + singular count noun + *that*

   SING. CN

   He had *so bad a headache that* he left early.

   b) *such* + *a* + adjective + singular count noun + *that*

   SING. CN

   He had *such a bad headache that* he left early.

NOTES:

   a. Be careful not to omit *a* before a singular count noun.

   b. The pattern of cause-and-result is expressed by *so/such . . . that*. Do *not* use *too* or *as*.

   *For problems with *many* and *much*, see *Modifiers—Few*, *Little*, *Much*, and *Many*, page 35.

ERROR EXAMPLES

A. WRONG: The doctor had too many patients that he could not see them all.

   RIGHT: The doctor had *so* many patients that he could not see them all.

B. WRONG: It was so good game that the stadium was packed.
    RIGHT: It was *such a good* game that the stadium was packed.

OR

It was *so good* a game that the stadium was packed.

C. WRONG: The book was as interesting that I could not put it down.
    RIGHT: The book was *so* interesting that I could not put it down.

D. WRONG: He is so shy as he never speaks in class.
    RIGHT: He is so shy *that* he never speaks in class.

E. WRONG: They had a such good time in Rome that they always dreamed of going back.
    RIGHT: They had *such a* good time in Rome that they always dreamed of going back.

F. WRONG: He gave me so good advice that I was very grateful to him.
    RIGHT: He gave me *such* good advice that I was very grateful to him.

EXERCISE: Put "C" if the sentence is correct. Put "X" if there is an error in the cause-and-result clause.

_____1. They had so a good meal at that restaurant that they wanted to go there again.

_____2. They were such talented actors that their movie was a great success.

_____3. The store had too few customers that it closed.

_____4. It was such a long lesson that we could not finish it in one day.

_____5. He was as rich that he owned four homes.

_____6. He is so forgetful as he never pays his rent on time.

_____7. She was such a good student that she won a scholarship.

_____8. They had a such bad day that they got depressed.

_____9. It was so warm weather that we went to the swimming pool.

_____10. The old woman's handwriting was so faint that I could hardly read it.

_____11. The stars are so far from the earth that we cannot see most of them.

_____12. I had too many things to do that I could not finish them all.

_____13. It was so confusing as I could not understand it.

_____14. He spoke such good Arabic that he surprised everyone.

_____15. The building was as large that we had difficulty finding his office.

Check your answers with the error key on page 71.

MODIFIERS—ARTICLES

1. Use *a* or *an* with an unspecified singular count noun.
    Use *an* before a word that begins with a vowel or a vowel sound.

    I saw *a puppy* in the park yesterday.

    The woman asked for *an exact* count.

    He is *an honest* man.

2. Use *the* with specified singular and plural count nouns.

    The puppy I saw in the park was black and white.

    The engineers from Clearwater Company designed a new system for water purification.

3. Do *not* use an article with plural count nouns used in a general sense.

    Dogs make good pets.

    Astronauts go through rigorous training programs to prepare for space flights.

4. Do *not* use an article with non-count nouns used in a general sense.

    I do not like *seafood*.

    Honesty is the best policy.

ERROR EXAMPLES

A. WRONG: We went to the store and bought new stove.
    RIGHT: We went to the store and bought *a* new stove.

B. WRONG: Everyone should have a equal opportunity to get an education.
    RIGHT: Everyone should have *an* equal opportunity to get an education.

C. WRONG: They had an accident in new car they bought last week.
    RIGHT: They had an accident in *the* new car they bought last week.

D. WRONG: It is traditional to have the flowers at a wedding.
    RIGHT: It is traditional *to have flowers* at a wedding.

E. WRONG: The honesty is a virtue.
    RIGHT: *Honesty* is a virtue.

EXERCISE: Put "C" if the sentence is correct. Put "X" if there is an article mistake.

_____1. John's friends had a farewell party for him last Friday.

_____2. He tried hard to get good grade on the test.

_____3. It is always difficult to make the decisions.

_____4. When he lived in Paris he went to parties every weekend.

_____5. They gave me a electric typewriter for my birthday.

_____6. Paul began to think that he would never find the happiness.

_____7. The old man no longer believed that money was the most important thing in life.

_____8. He wanted to try on pair of jogging shoes at the shoe store.

_____9. In all his life he had never wanted to try the wine.

_____10. She does not have an understanding of the subject yet.

_____11. I just saw boys from Africa that I met at the International House party last week.

_____12. Teachers usually spend many hours correcting papers.

_____13. Some people believe that the frankness is the best policy in any situation.

_____14. The man who fixed my air-conditioning unit accidentally broke the fan.

_____15. The doctors have to go to school for many years to complete their education.

Check your answers with the error key on page 71.

MODIFIERS—*TOO, VERY,* AND *ENOUGH*

Compare the meanings and patterns of *too*, *very*, and *enough*:

1. *Very* means *to a high degree*, but does not suggest impossibility or undesirability.

    VERY + ADJ.
    Mary is *very intelligent*.

2. *Too* suggests *impossibility* or *undesirable degree*.

    TOO + ADJ. + TO + V
    She is *too sick to come* to class today.

3. *Enough* suggests *possibility* or *sufficient degree*.

    ADJ. + ENOUGH + TO + V
    He is *tall enough to play* basketball.

NOTES:

   a. Be careful to put *enough* AFTER the adjective.

   b. Be careful to put <u>to</u> + V (infinitive) AFTER *enough*.

   c. In patterns 2 and 3 above, do not use any other structure-word after the adjective or adverb except *to*.

   d. In the above patterns adverbs can be used in the same position as adjectives. Example: Mary sings *very well*.

   e. *Enough* can come before or after a noun to express sufficiency.

He had *money enough* to buy a new car.

OR

He had *enough money* to buy a new car.

ERROR EXAMPLES

A. WRONG: This meat is too delicious.
   RIGHT: This meat is *very* delicious.

B. WRONG: It was very late to catch the plane.
   RIGHT: It was *too* late to catch the plane.

C. WRONG: He was enough old to get a driver's license.
   RIGHT: He was *old enough* to get a driver's license.

D. WRONG: His English was enough good as for him to pass the TOEFL.
   RIGHT: His English was *good enough* for him to pass the TOEFL.

E. WRONG: We had very much time to finish our work.
   RIGHT: We had *enough time* to finish our work.

EXERCISE: Put "C" if the sentence is correct. Put "X" if there is an error with *too*, *very*, or *enough*.

_____1. I had enough experience to get the job.

_____2. This soup is too good.

_____3. It was too late to go to the theater.

_____4. He is enough intelligent to do well in school.

_____5. Paul had very much money to buy a new motorcycle.

_____6. I am very disappointed in his behavior.

_____7. He made too many good friends when he studied abroad.

_____8. She spoke French well enough to be a translator.

_____9. He did not speak English as well enough to be understood.

_____10. The envelope was thin enough to slide under the door.

_____11. The sofa was big enough as to seat four people comfortably.

_____12. This paragraph is not enough good as to be acceptable.

_____13. His TOEFL score was high enough to be accepted.

_____14. She was too happy when she heard the news.

_____15. She was enough old to get married.

Check your answers with the error key on page 72.

MODIFIERS—NEGATION

1. *Not* is an adverb that negates verbs. *Not* is used in the following patterns:

     a)   auxiliary + *not* + V + ing

         AUX. + NOT + V + -ING
         He *is not going* to the party.

         AUX. + NOT + V + -ING
         He *is not making* any money.

     b)   auxiliary + *not* + V

         AUX. + NOT + V
         He *does not like* to study on the weekends.

         AUX. + NOT + V
         We *do not want* any coffee, thank you.

     c)   auxiliary + *not* + past participle

         AUX. + NOT + PAST PART.
         He *has not been* here for days.

         AUX. + NOT + PAST PART.
         They *have not seen* any deer.

    *d)   modal + *not* + V

         MODAL + NOT + V
         We *will not accept* your opinion.

         MODAL + NOT + V
         You *should not eat* too many sweets.

2. *No* is an adjective that indicates the absence of something. It modifies nouns. It is used in the following pattern:

Verb + *no* + noun

V + NO + N
There *is no charge* for towels at the pool.

V + NO + N
He *has no passport.*

3. *None* is a pronoun meaning *not any* or *not one.* Use *none* when the noun it replaces has been mentioned already.

The children ate all the *cookies.* When I arrived, there

PRON.
were *none.* (*none* = no cookies)

PRON.
They asked me to contribute some *money* but I had *none.*
(*none* = no money)

None may also be used in the following pattern:

None + *of the* + noun

In this pattern, the noun that *none* refers to is placed after *of the.*

PRON. + OF THE + N
When I arrived, *none of the cookies* were left.

PRON. + OF THE + N
None of the children know how to swim.

4. Remember to use *any* after negative words to express the absence of quantity for plural count nouns and non-count nouns. [*Anyone, anybody, anywhere, anymore* and *anything* can also be used in negative sentence constructions.]

NEG.   ANY   NCN
I do *not* have *any free time* today.

NEG. ANY   PL. CN
There were *not any students* from China this year.

NEG.   ANYMORE
He does *not* go to school *anymore.*

NEG.   ANYONE
We did *not* see *anyone* leave the building.

5. There are some words that have negative meanings even though they do not appear to be negative, for example: *hardly*, *scarcely*, *rarely*, *seldom*, *without*, and *only*. Do not use another negative word with these words. (See notes.)

NEG.

He had *scarcely* enough money for the bus.

NEG.

They went to bed *without* dinner.

6. Negative infinitives (*to* + V) are formed by putting *not* before the infinitive (*not* + *to* + V).

NOT + TO + V

She said *not to talk* during the program.

NOT + TO + V

They told us to relax and *not to worry*.

7. Remember that *no longer* is an idiomatic negative expression of time.

He *no longer* lives here.

They *no longer* play golf together.

NOTES:

a. To express a negative idea, use only one negative word. Two negative words in one sentence make the sentence an affirmative statement, for example, "Do *not* leave *without* an umbrella." ("Be sure to take your umbrella.")

b. Never use *not longer* when *longer* means time.

*For an explanation of modals, see *Verbs—Modals*, page 85.

ERROR EXAMPLES

A. WRONG: He is no going on vacation this summer.
    RIGHT: He is *not* going on vacation this summer.

B. WRONG: There is not butter in the refrigerator.
    RIGHT: There is *no* butter in the refrigerator.

C. WRONG: There were none children in the playground.
    RIGHT: There were *no* children in the playground.

D. WRONG: We do not have no class Friday.
   RIGHT: We do not have *any* class Friday.

E. WRONG: They seldom do not go to the movies.
   RIGHT: They *seldom go* to the movies.

F. WRONG: I encourage you to do not wait for him.
   RIGHT: I encourage you *not to wait* for him.

G. WRONG: She said to sit quietly and to not open our books.
   RIGHT: She said to sit quietly and *not to open* our books.

H. WRONG: He ran out of money and could not longer continue school.
   RIGHT: He ran out of money and could *no* longer continue school.

I. WRONG: The children went to the movies without no money.
   RIGHT: The children went to the movies without *any* money.

J. WRONG: I searched all day for some new shoes, but there were none shoes I liked.
   RIGHT: I searched all day for some new shoes, but there were *none* I liked.

EXERCISE: Put "C" if the sentence is correct. Put "X" if there is an error in negation.

_____1. He could not lend me $5 because he did not have only $3.

_____2. There were several of his friends at the restaurant, but none of mine came.

_____3. The rules required us to form an orderly line and to do not talk.

_____4. None of the shoes on sale fit me.

_____5. You are no going to finish the test in time.

_____6. Rarely does one see such a handsome man.

_____7. He could not longer tolerate that situation.

_____8. There were not cheaper beds left at that furniture store.

_____9. The director told the chorus to sit down and not to whisper.

_____10. By the time I arrived, there was no birthday cake left.

_____11. He could not scarcely believe what I told him.

_____12. That couple has none children.

_____13. Do not go to the mountains without no sturdy hiking boots.

_____14. We were no interested in what they were selling.

_____15. No longer can the world afford to waste its natural resources.

_____16. He did not have no good reason for hitting him.

_____17. If I were you I would no take that course.

_____18. The Smiths could afford to pay only $40,000 for a new home, and they were quite dismayed to learn that there were none available in that price range.

_____19. The children could not hardly believe their eyes when they saw a giraffe for the first time.

_____20. They foolishly drove into the desert without any extra water.

Check your answers with the error key on page 72.

CHAPTER QUIZ—Modifiers

DIRECTIONS: Each of the following sentences has four underlined words or phrases, one of which contains an error that is not acceptable in standard written English. Write the letter of the error in the space provided. (When taking the TOEFL, use the answer sheet provided and follow the directions).

_____1. He found an interesting lithograph <u>as</u> the <u>one</u> he <u>had seen</u>
                                                 A   B   C

       <u>on</u> his trip to Spain.
       D

_____2. I told him as <u>forceful</u> as possible <u>that</u> he would not
                       A   B

       <u>be allowed</u> to enter the room without <u>written</u> permission.
       C   D

_____3. Dr. Fields received <u>so large bill</u> when he checked out of the
                              A

       hotel <u>that</u> he did <u>not</u> have <u>enough money</u> to pay for a taxi
             B   C   D
       to the airport.

_____4. Although David had <u>originally</u> agreed to help her, he later
                           A

       decided it <u>would be</u> more time-consuming <u>that</u> he
                 B   C

       <u>had anticipated</u>.
       D

_____5. The hunters were able to <u>take</u> their limit of <u>game</u> with <u>few</u>
                          A   B   C

       effort <u>in spite of</u> the unusually rainy weather.
             D

_____6. <u>In spite of</u> the wonderful acting, sensitive photography, and
       A

       <u>well-developed</u> plot, the <u>three-hours</u> movie <u>could</u> not hold
       B   C   D
       our attention.

_____7. The weatherman <u>suggests</u> <u>keeping</u> small children out of
                        A   B

the sun because he predicts <u>that</u> today will be <u>hottest</u> day
                              C   D

of the year.

_____8. The American businessmen were perplexed by the <u>much</u>
                                                            A

considerations that the foreign company <u>had to</u> take into
                                          B

account before <u>arriving</u> <u>at</u> a decision.
                  C   D

_____9. The new zoo, with <u>its</u> elaborate moat system and open
                            A

spaces, <u>was</u> <u>enough roomy</u> to accommodate <u>even</u> very
          B   C   D

large animals comfortably.

_____10. All of the players <u>were anticipating</u> the last game of the
                                A

series, <u>which</u> they expected <u>to be</u> <u>real</u> exciting.
          B   C   D

_____11. <u>Having given</u> serious consideration to a job offer from
            A

another company, Bob finally decided to <u>completely</u> forget
                                          B

about the offer and <u>to continue</u> <u>at</u> his old job.
                      C   D

_____12. I <u>scarcely have</u> <u>enough</u> money <u>to pay</u> the bill I <u>received</u>
              A   B   C   D

for medical services.

_____13. After <u>having dinner</u> in that restaurant last night, I felt <u>badly</u>
                  A   B

and my wife <u>had</u> <u>to take</u> me to the hospital.
              C   D

_____14. <u>Before leaving</u> for her <u>two-week</u> vacation, Sharon had to
            A   B

<u>quickly</u> prepare the monthly <u>financial</u> report.
  C   D

_____15.   A prize was awarded to millionth person who bought a
                    A   B   C

year's subscription to the magazine.
D

_____16.   Although Niagara Falls in the United States is not as high
                                        A

than Angel Falls in Venezuela, more tourists visit Niagara
B

Falls because it is more accessible .
                    C   D

_____17.   Seriously burned in a terrible car accident, the doctor was
                    A

not sure that John could be protected from infection
                            B

long enough for his body to begin to heal itself .
C   D

_____18.   My friend Dorothy, who just got back from Paris, said that
                            A   B

the view from the top of the Eiffel Tower was too
                                              C   D

breathtaking.

_____19.   After a long, seemingly futile search, Professor Clayborne
                            A

was finally able to locate the five volume of the series he
        B   C

needed to continue his research.
        D

_____20.   They only publish stories that are suitable for young
                A   B   C

children to read .
            D

_____21.   Because of the long, detailed questions and the unfamiliar
        A   B

format, John could not scarcely finish the test on time .
                C   D

_____22. Clark spent <u>many</u> years <u>studying</u> Eastern philosophy <u>in</u>
                    A   B   C

his search for the meaning of <u>the life</u>.
                              D

_____23. Although he <u>had scaled</u> many of the <u>world's</u> tallest moun-
                        A   B

tains, he was still <u>looking for</u> <u>more taller</u> peaks to climb.
                    C   D

_____24. The mechanic <u>recently</u> purchased <u>these</u> set of tools
                        A   B

<u>in order to</u> be able to work <u>on</u> large diesel trucks.
    C   D

_____25. We all looked forward <u>to</u> <u>going</u> on our <u>class's</u> picnic <u>on</u>
                              A   B   C   D

the last day of the semester.

_____26. They were <u>completely</u> unprepared for the difficulties of
                    A

<u>caring</u> for a <u>three-months-old</u> baby <u>on</u> their European trip.
    B   C   D

_____27. <u>Driving</u> across the bridge, the sailboat with <u>its</u> sails
        A   B

<u>billowing</u> in the wind <u>was</u> a beautiful sight to see.
    C   D

_____28. They could not help <u>noticing</u> <u>the</u> article posted about <u>a</u>
                            A   B   C

unusual flying object seen <u>recently</u>.
                          D

_____29. <u>Even though</u> my friend considered a career in economics
        A

or business administration, he <u>finally</u> decided <u>on</u> a <u>physic</u>
                              B   C   D

major.

_____30. <u>As</u> he was driving me home, he told me <u>that</u> he <u>not longer</u>
        A   B   C

spent his winters <u>in</u> Florida.
                D

Check your answers with the error key on page 73.

ERROR KEYS

MODIFIERS—Adverbs Like ONLY

ERROR KEY

  C 1.

  C 2.

  X 3. (*hardly* any English). *Hardly* modifies *any*.

  X 4. (*almost* twenty dollars). *Almost* modifies *twenty*.

  C 5.

  X 6. (*hardly* enough time). *Hardly* modifies *enough*.

  C 7.

  X 8. (*scarcely* five hours). *Scarcely* modifies *five*.

  C 9.

  X 10. (*only* one person). *Only* modifies *one*.

MODIFIERS—Split Infinitives

ERROR KEY

  C 1.

  X 2. (*to understand the situation easily*)

  X 3. (*To make him really happy*)

  X 4. (*to weigh the vegetables accurately*)

  X 5. (*to finish your homework completely*)

  X 6. (*To read the material hastily*)

  C 7.

  X 8. (*to revise your work entirely*)

  C 9.

  X 10. (*to decide soon*)

MODIFIERS—Dangling Modifiers

ERROR KEY

__X__ 1.   (Playing in the street, *the child was hit by the truck*).

__X__ 2.   (By painting and repairing as needed, *one can keep one's home in good condition*).

__C__ 3.

__X__ 4.   (*After I had addressed and stamped the letter, I dropped it in the slot*).

__C__ 5.

__X__ 6.   (Walking toward the church, *I noticed the beautiful stained-glass windows*).

__X__ 7.   (To understand the subject, *one must do a great deal of studying*).

__X__ 8.   (Skiing down the steep hill, *I felt my heart beat crazily*).

__C__ 9.

__C__ 10.

__X__ 11.   (*When I was only a child*, my father taught me how to play soccer).

__X__ 12.   (Studying and reading, *I passed the day quickly*).

__C__ 13.

__X__ 14.   (Sitting alone in his room, *he was frightened by the strange noise*).

__X__ 15.   (*Having wrapped the package in pretty green paper, Phyllis put it on the table*).

MODIFIERS—Adjective/Adverb Confusion

ERROR KEY

__X__ 1.   (*late*). See note b.

__C__ 2.

__C__ 3.

__C__ 4.   Note: In this sentence, the adverb *exquisitely* modifies the adjective *carved*; however, a similar sentence could be constructed using the adjective *exquisite* to modify the noun *vase* (. . . an exquisite, carved vase).

___X___ 5. (*really* good chance). See rule 3.

___C___ 6.

___C___ 7.

___X___ 8. (*hastily* called). See rule 3.

___X___ 9. (*thoroughly* interested). See rule 3.

___C___ 10.

___X___ 11. (to arrive *promptly*). See rule 2.

___C___ 12.

___C___ 13.

___X___ 14. (*fast*). See note b.

___X___ 15. (really *well*). See rule 2 and note c.

___X___ 16. (*carefully* organized). See rule 3.

___C___ 17.

___X___ 18. (plays tennis *badly*). See rule 2.

___C___ 19.

___X___ 20. (very *fast*). See note b.

MODIFIERS—Adjectives After Verbs of Sensation

ERROR KEY

___X___ 1. (*sad*)

___C___ 2.

___X___ 3. (*awful*)

___C___ 4.

___X___ 5. (*loud*)

___C___ 6.

___X___ 7. (*nice*)

___X___ 8. (*sour*)

___C___ 9.

___X___ 10. (*nervous*)

MODIFIERS—Noun Adjectives

ERROR KEY

__X__ 1. (*police* station). See note a.

__C__ 2.

__X__ 3. (*car* license). See note a.

__X__ 4. (*street* lights). See note a.

__X__ 5. (an *economics* class). See note b.

__X__ 6. (*world* situation). See note a.

__C__ 7.

__C__ 8.

__X__ 9. (*football* teams). See note a.

__C__ 10.

__C__ 11.

__X__ 12. (*dormitory* rules). See note a.

__C__ 13.

__X__ 14. (*television* repairman). See note a.

__X__ 15. (*dance* recitals). See note a.

__C__ 16.

__X__ 17. (*plane* ticket). See note a.

__X__ 18. (*language* courses). See note a.

__C__ 19.

__X__ 20. (*physics* course). See note b.

MODIFIERS—Hyphenated or Compound Adjectives

ERROR KEY

__C__ 1.

__X__ 2. (thirty-*year*-old man)

__X__ 3. (five-*dollar*-a-pound cheese)

__C__ 4.

_X_ 5. (five-thousand-*year*-old pyramids)

_X_ 6. (two-*ounce* bottle)

_C_ 7.

_C_ 8.

_X_ 9. (five-hundred-*page* manual)

_X_ 10. (ten-*room* house)

MODIFIERS—Demonstratives

ERROR KEY

_C_ 1.

_X_ 2. (*this* class)

_C_ 3.

_C_ 4.

_X_ 5. (these *kinds*)

_X_ 6. (those *kinds*)

_C_ 7.

_X_ 8. (*this* pair)

_X_ 9. (*these* movies)

_C_ 10.

MODIFIERS—FEW, LITTLE, MUCH, and MANY

ERROR KEY

_X_ 1. (*much* sugar). See rule 2.

_C_ 2.

_C_ 3.

_X_ 4. (*least* medical attention). See rule 2.

_X_ 5. (*little* news). See rule 2 and note c.

_C_ 6.

C 7.

C 8.

X 9. (the *fewest* cavities). See rule 1.

X 10. (*little* money). See rule 2.

C 11.

X 12. (*many* women). See rule 1 and note a.

C 13.

X 14. (*much* news). See rule 2 and note c.

X 15. (*less* information). See rule 2.

X 16. (a *few* people). See rule 1 and note a.

X 17. (*much* homework). See rule 2 and note b.

C 18.

X 19. (*many* campus police). See rule 1 and note a.

X 20. (*much* fruit). See rule 1 and note b.

MODIFIERS—Cardinal and Ordinal Numbers

ERROR KEY

C 1.

X 2. (in *line fifteen*). See rule 2 and note b.

X 3. (Do *exercise one*). See rule 2 and note b. OR (Do *the first exercise*). See rule 1.

X 4. (at teller *four*). See rule 2. OR (the *fourth* teller). See rule 1.

C 5.

X 6. (at *the third* window). See rule 1. OR (at *window three*). See rule 2.

C 7.

X 8. (in *the first* aisle). See rule 1. OR (in *aisle one*). See rule 2.

C 9.

X 10. (on *page six*). See rule 2.

MODIFIERS—Sameness and Similarity

ERROR KEY

_X_ 1. (*like* the one). See rule 1.

_C_ 2.

_X_ 3. (*as* mine). See rule 2.

_X_ 4. (as beautiful *as*). See rule 3.

_C_ 5.

_C_ 6.

_X_ 7. (*like* her mother). See rule 1.

_X_ 8. (the same *price* as). See rule 2. OR (*as* expensive as). See rule 3.

_C_ 9.

_X_ 10. (as intelligent *as*). See rule 3.

_C_ 11.

_C_ 12.

_X_ 13. (style *as*). See rule 2.

_C_ 14.

_X_ 15. (color *as*). See rule 2.

MODIFIERS—Comparatives

ERROR KEY

_X_ 1. (is *better* than). See note a.

_X_ 2. (higher *than*). See rule 4 and note b.

_C_ 3.

_C_ 4.

_X_ 5. (was *friendlier* than). See note a.

_X_ 6. (happier than *anybody else* in her family). See error example G.

_C_ 7.

_C_ 8.

X   9. (much hotter this year than *that* in 1970.). See error examples E and F.

.C   10.

X   11. (more crowded *than* the second one). See rule 4 and note b.

C   12.

C   13.

X   14. (any *other* house). See error examples G and H.

X   15. (hurt *worse* than). See rule 3.

MODIFIERS—Superlatives

ERROR KEY

X   1. (*the poorest* people). See note b.

C   2.

X   3. (the most surprised person *of all the contestants.*). See note c.

X   4. (Belgium *the best*). See note d.

C   5.

X   6. (*the* hottest and *the* most humid month). See note a.

X   7. (*the biggest* building). See note b.

C   8.

X   9. (doctor *that*). See note c.

C   10.

X   11. (*the most* elegant). See note d.

X   12. (*the* most densely). See note a.

X   13. (the worst *that*). See note c.

C   14.

X   15. (the fastest runner *on the team*). See note c.

C   16.

X   17. (the *best* ice cream). See rule 3.

C   18.

X   19. (the *worst* grade). See rule 3.

C   20.

MODIFIERS—Cause and Result

ERROR KEY

___X___ 1. (so good *a* meal) OR (*such* a good meal). See rule 3.

___C___ 2.

___X___ 3. (had *so* few customers that). See note b.

___C___ 4.

___X___ 5. (was *so* rich that). See note b.

___X___ 6. (so forgetful *that*). See note b.

___C___ 7.

___X___ 8. (had *such* a bad day that) OR (had so bad *a* day that). See rule 3.

___X___ 9. (was *such* warm weather that). See rule 2b.

___C___ 10.

___C___ 11.

___X___ 12. (had *so* many things to do that). See note b.

___X___ 13. (so confusing *that*). See note b.

___C___ 14.

___X___ 15. (*so* large that). See note b.

MODIFIERS—Articles

ERROR KEY

___C___ 1.

___X___ 2. (*a* good grade). See rule 1.

___X___ 3. (*to make decisions*). See rule 3.

___C___ 4.

___X___ 5. (*an* electric typewriter). See rule 1.

___X___ 6. (*find happiness*). See rule 4.

___C___ 7.

___X___ 8. (on *a* pair of jogging shoes). See rule 1.

___X___ 9. (*to try wine*). See rule 4.

_C_ 10.

_X_ 11. (saw *the* boys). See rule 2.

_C_ 12.

_X_ 13. (*that frankness* is). See rule 4.

_C_ 14.

_X_ 15. (*Doctors* have to go). See rule 3.

MODIFIERS—TOO, VERY, and ENOUGH

ERROR KEY

_C_ 1.

_X_ 2. (*very* good). See rule 1.

_C_ 3.

_X_ 4. (*intelligent enough*). See note a.

_X_ 5. (had *enough* money). See rule 3.

_C_ 6.

_X_ 7. (made *many* good friends). See rule 2.

_C_ 8.

_X_ 9. (English *well* enough). See rule 3 and note c.

_C_ 10.

_X_ 11. (big *enough to* seat). See rule 2 and note c.

_X_ 12. (*good enough* to). See note a and note c.

_C_ 13.

_X_ 14. (*very* happy). See rule 1.

_X_ 15. (*old enough*). See note a.

MODIFIERS—Negation

ERROR KEY

_X_ 1. (he *had* only $3). See rule 5.

_C_ 2.

_X_ 3. (and *not to talk*). See rule 6.

_C_ 4.

_X_ 5. (are *not* going to). See rule 1.

_C_ 6.

_X_ 7. (*no* longer). See rule 7.

_X_ 8. (*no* cheaper beds). See rule 2.

_C_ 9.

_C_ 10.

_X_ 11. (*could scarcely*). See rule 5.

_X_ 12. (*no* children). See rule 2.

_X_ 13. (*without sturdy* hiking boots). See rule 5.

_X_ 14. (were *not* interested). See rule 1.

_C_ 15.

_X_ 16. (did not have *any* good reason). See rule 4.

_X_ 17. (would *not* take). See rule 1.

_C_ 18.

_X_ 19. (*could hardly* believe). See rule 5.

_C_ 20.

CHAPTER QUIZ—Modifiers

ERROR KEY

_A_ 1. See *Sameness and Similarity*, page 39.

_A_ 2. See *Adjective/Adverb Confusion*, page 27.

_A_ 3. See *Cause and Result*, page 47.

_C_ 4. See *Comparatives*, page 41.

_C_ 5. See *Few*, *Little*, *Much*, and *Many*, page 35.

_C_ 6. See *Hyphenated or Compound Adjectives*, page 33.

_D_ 7. See *Superlatives*, page 44.

_A_ 8. See *Few*, *Little*, *Much*, and *Many*, page 35.

_C_ 9. See *Too*, *Very*, and *Enough*, page 52.

  D 10. See *Adjective/Adverb Confusion*, page 27.

  B 11. See *Split Infinitives*, page 24.

  A 12. See *Adverbs like <u>Only</u>*, page 23.

  B 13. See *Adjectives After Verbs of Sensation*, page 30.

  C 14. See *Split Infinitives*, page 24.

  B 15. See *Cardinal and Ordinal Numbers*, page 38.

  B 16. See *Sameness and Similarity*, page 39.

  A 17. See *Dangling Modifiers*, page 25.

  D 18. See *<u>Too</u>, <u>Very</u>, and <u>Enough</u>*, page 52.

  C 19. See *Cardinal and Ordinal Numbers*, page 38.

  A 20. See *Adverbs like <u>Only</u>*, page 23.

  C 21. See *Negation*, page 54.

  D 22. See *Articles*, page 50.

  D 23. See *Comparatives*, page 41.

  B 24. See *Demonstratives*, page 34.

  C 25. See *Noun Adjectives*, page 31.

  C 26. See *Hyphenated or Compound Adjectives*, page 33.

  A 27. See *Dangling Modifiers*, page 25.

  C 28. See *Articles*, page 50.

  D 29. See *Noun Adjectives*, page 31.

  C 30. See *Negation*, page 54.

IX

VERBS

VERBS—TENSE

The following are common verb-tense problems:

1. *Present Perfect.* Remember to use the present perfect *only* when the action has started in the past and still relates to the present.

>   I *have been* in the United States for six months.

>   She *has played* the piano since she was a child.

2. *Past Tense.* Remember to use the past tense when the action occurred or existed in the past.

>   I *went* to California last summer.

>   He *visited* several museums in Spain.

3. *Past Perfect.* Remember to use the past perfect only to express an activity that happened before another past activity.

>   The movie *had begun* when we arrived.

>   I *had* already *left* when he called.

Note: It is possible to use the past perfect in sentences where *before* or *after* show sequence, but it is not necessary.

ERROR EXAMPLES

A. WRONG: I have finished a game of tennis with John when Bob arrived.

   RIGHT: I *had finished* a game of tennis with John when Bob arrived.

B. WRONG: Since Bob graduated last year, he had been traveling around Europe.
    RIGHT: Since Bob graduated last year, he *has been traveling* around Europe.

C. WRONG: It has taken me a long time to do the homework last night.
    RIGHT: It *took* me a long time to do the homework last night.

D. WRONG: Since 1976 he is living in Brazil.
    RIGHT: Since 1976 he *has been living* in Brazil.

OR

Since 1976 he *has lived* in Brazil.

EXERCISE: Put "C" if the sentence is correct. Put "X" if there is an error in the verb tense.

_____1. I have been in Mexico during the summer of 1970.

_____2. Mary had prepared dinner when I arrived, so we were able to eat immediately.

_____3. Three years ago he had been a student at a university in California.

_____4. We have collected stamps for many years.

_____5. We took the bus downtown, did a few errands, and had gone to lunch.

_____6. Since he bought a new car, he has been driving to work every day.

_____7. Last night they have recognized us from the party we went to earlier in the week.

_____8. Since Ted graduated, he has been working with his father.

_____9. The doctor had seen ten patients since eight o'clock this morning.

_____10. He is studying English for the last five years.

Check your answers with the error key on page 100.

VERBS—TIME CLAUSES

Use the simple present tense in future-time clauses (when the action will take place sometime in the future). (Never use *will* or *going to* in future-time clauses.) Time clauses* are introduced by such words as: *when*, *while*, *after*, *before*, *as soon as*, etc. See also *Verbs—Conditionals*, page 82.

    a) Future-time clauses:

<u>As soon as they *get* their degrees</u>, they are going home.

PRES

FUTURE-TIME CL.

<u>When I *see* him</u>, I will give him your message.

PRES

FUTURE-TIME CL.

*Other tenses may also be used in time clauses, but the present tense *must* be used in future-time clauses when the main clause is in the future.

ERROR EXAMPLES

A. WRONG: Whenever you will be in town, call me.
   RIGHT: Whenever you *are* in town, call me.

B. WRONG: As soon as I will get all the vaccinations I will need, I will be leaving for Southeast Asia.
   RIGHT: As soon as I *get* all the vaccinations I need, I will be leaving for Southeast Asia.

C. WRONG: After Dave is going to break the track record, many universities will offer him scholarships.
   RIGHT: After Dave *breaks* the track record, many universities will offer him scholarships.

EXERCISE: Put "C" if the sentence is correct. Put "X" if there is a mistake in the time clause.

_____1. You should visit that part of the country when it will be spring.

_____2. It will get cold in the desert when winter will come.

_____3. As soon as you learn to swim, I will take you to our cabin at the lake.

_____4. When the children are going to visit their grandmother, Henry and I will be going to Europe.

_____5. When Bruce visits him tomorrow, his doctor will probably tell him to increase his medication.

_____6. Will you buy me a wool jacket when you will be in Scotland?

_____7. The actress who plays this role will receive an award when the critics will see her performance.

_____8. When I have time, I will try to run two miles.

_____9. When the fire engines go down the street, all the dogs in the neighborhood howl.

_____10. As soon as Joan will get a good job, she is going to buy a condominium.

Check your answers with the error key on page 100.

VERBS—VERBS OF "DEMAND"

The simple verb (V) is used for all persons in a noun clause after the following verbs:

demand	recommend	be necessary
insist	urge	be required
require	advise	be essential
suggest	request	be important
	ask (when it means *request*)	

The doctor recommended that she *have*^V surgery.

I suggest that he *be*^V ready on time.

She asked that all employees *attend*^V the meeting.

NOTE:

Use *not* to make the verb negative. Do not use *don't*.

NOT + V

The weatherman suggested that people *not use* Highway 7.

ERROR EXAMPLES

A. WRONG: The doctor advised that I am going on a diet.
    RIGHT: The doctor advised that I *go* on a diet.

B. WRONG: The restaurant suggested that we arrived on time for our reservation.
    RIGHT: The restaurant suggested that we *arrive* on time for our reservation.

C. WRONG: The instructions ask that we don't use a red pen.
    RIGHT: The instructions ask that we *not use* a red pen.

D. WRONG: The law requires that students are in school a certain number of days a year.
    RIGHT: The law requires that students *be* in school a certain number of days a year.

E. WRONG: It was important that money was collected for the cause.
    RIGHT: It was important that money *be* collected for the cause.

EXERCISE: Put "C" if the sentence is correct. Put "X" if there is an error in the verb in the noun clause after a "demand" verb.

_____1.   The supervisor recommended that all employees took a course in speed reading.

_____2.   They request that you be fluent in Spanish.

_____3.   My doctor urges that I am stopping smoking immediately.

_____4.   It was essential that the train leave on time.

_____5.   The professor advised that John had a private tutor for a few weeks.

_____6.   The admiral demanded that his crew has inspection twice a day.

_____7.   They asked that she not call before 8:00 A.M.

_____8. The gracious hosts insisted that Mr. Smith did not leave so early.

_____9. I suggested that he wear black for the ceremony.

_____10. The police require that a driver renews his license every three years.

Check your answers with the error key on page 101.

VERBS—WISHES

1. *Present* wishes are expressed in the *past* tense.

> PAST
> Ralph wishes that he *had* $1,000,000.   (but he doesn't)

> PAST
> Mary wishes that she *lived* in New York.   (but she doesn't)

> PAST
> Grace wishes that she *did not have* a test tomorrow.
> (but she does)

2. Always use *were* in present wishes for *to be*.

> He has often wished that he *were* older.   (but he's not).
>
> I often wish that I *were* in Hawaii.   (but I'm not)
>
> We often wish that we *were not* so busy.   (but we are)
>
> They often wish that they *were not* living in Chicago.
> (but they are)

3. *Past* wishes are expressed in the *past perfect*.

> PAST PERF.
> Hiromi wishes that she *had studied* more English before arriving in the United States.   (but she didn't)

PAST PERF.

Kathy and Bob wish that they *had gotten* married before she went to Africa.   (but they didn't)

PAST PERF.

The children wish they *had not disobeyed* their mother. (but they did)

NOTE:

After the verb *wish*, the noun clause may be introduced by the conjunction *that*.

ERROR EXAMPLES

A. WRONG: Steven wishes that he has a bigger apartment.
    RIGHT: Steven wishes that he *had* a bigger apartment.

B. WRONG: Helen wishes that she does not live in a dormitory.
    RIGHT: Helen wishes that she *did not* live in a dormitory.

C. WRONG: The actor wishes he was not required to perform every evening.
    RIGHT: The actor wishes he *were* not required to perform every evening.

D. WRONG: Ted wishes that he did not lose his job last month.
    RIGHT: Ted wishes that he *had not lost* his job last month.

E. WRONG: Bob wishes that he bought that house last spring.
    RIGHT: Bob wishes that he *had bought* that house last spring.

F. WRONG: I wish that I was living in a warmer climate.
    RIGHT: I wish that I *were* living in a warmer climate.

EXERCISE: Put "C" if the sentence is correct. Put "X" if there is an error in the verb that expresses a wish.

_____1.   They wish they were able to spend more time in London.

_____2.   My father wishes that he does not have to retire at age sixty-five.

_____3.   The farmer wished that he does not lose money on his cotton crop.

_____4.   Abdulla wishes that his soccer team were the national champions.

_____ 5. The doctor wishes that he has more free time to play golf.

_____ 6. Each of her children wishes that he did not ignore the advice that she gave him.

_____ 7. I wish that I was earning more money and working less time.

_____ 8. My mother wishes that my father does more work around the house.

_____ 9. We wish that we did not have to go to the library this Saturday.

_____ 10. My friend Dorothy wishes she was still living in Paris.

Check your answers with the error key on page 101.

VERBS—CONDITIONALS

There are two kinds of conditions—real and unreal:

1. *Real* conditions are used for *possible* situations. The present tense is used in the *if*-clause (or conditional clause), and the future tense is used in the result clause.

>   PRES.   FUT.
>   If he *comes* to school, I *will give* him your message.
>   (It is possible that he will come.)

2. *Unreal* conditions are used for *impossible* or *unreal* situations.

    a) In present time the past tense is used in the *if*-clause and *would*, *could*, or *might*, + the simple verb (V) is used in the result clause.

    >   PAST   COULD + V
    >   If he *studied*, he *could get* good grades.
    >   (He doesn't study.)

    >   PAST   WOULD + V
    >   If he *came* to school, I *would give* him your message.
    >   (He doesn't come to school.)

b) In past time the past perfect is used in the *if*-clause, and *would*, *could*, or *might* + *have* + the past participle are used in the result clause.

PAST PERF.   WOULD + HAVE + PAST PART.

If he *had come* to school, I *would have given* him your message.

(He didn't come to school.)

SUMMARY: *If* + present . . . . future (result)
                 If + past . . . . *would* + V (result)
                 If + past perfect . . . . . . *would* + *have* + past part. (result)

NOTES:

a. In general, avoid using *would* in the *if*-clause.

b. In present-time unreal *if*-clauses, the correct form of the verb *to be* for all persons is *were*.

If he *were* rich, he would go to Europe to study.

If I *were* you, I would study harder.

ERROR EXAMPLES

A. WRONG: If I will win the contest, I will buy a new car.
      RIGHT: If I *win* the contest, I will buy a new car.

B. WRONG: If you had lost your job, what would you do?
      RIGHT: If you *lost* your job, what would you do?

OR

If you had lost your job, what *would* you *have done*?

C. WRONG: If I had been there, I would make a speech.
      RIGHT: If I *were* there, I would make a speech.

OR

If I had been there, I *would have made* a speech.

D. WRONG: If they had ask me, I would have given them my opinion.
      RIGHT: If they had *asked* me, I would have given them my opinion.

E. WRONG: If Bob had studied more, he would have pass the test.
      RIGHT: If Bob had studied more, he would have *passed* the test.

F.   WRONG: If Jane had known it was supposed to rain, she would have took an umbrella.

      RIGHT: If Jane had known it was supposed to rain, she would have *taken* an umbrella.

G.   WRONG: If I would have a degree from that university, I would get a good job.

      RIGHT: If I *had* a degree from that university, I would get a good job.

H.   WRONG: If he would have been on time, we would have asked him to the party.

      RIGHT: If he *had been* on time, we would have asked him to the party.

EXERCISE: Put "C" if the sentence is correct. Put "X" if there is an error in the use of the conditional.

_____1.   If he had not tried to jump over the stream, he would not break his leg.

_____2.   If he would be taller, he would be a good basketball player.

_____3.   If my apartment would be larger, I would not have to move.

_____4.   If he was ready, we would begin the lesson.

_____5.   If classes had finished sooner, I would go to Canada last month.

_____6.   If Betty would have driven more carefully, she would not have had that accident.

_____7.   If I will finish studying, I will go to the movies with you.

_____8.   If the king had known the truth, he would have been very angry.

_____9.   If Bob had practiced playing tennis more, he will not have lost the game.

_____10.   If he had been here earlier, I would have saw him.

_____11.   If I had seen him, I would have reminded him about his appointment.

_____12.   If you will take a trip this summer, where will you go?

_____13.   If Bob·had received his check on time, he had certainly bought a new suit.

_____14.   If she were the only person available, we would have to hire her.

_____15. If she had told me that she did not have enough money,
I would pay for her trip last summer.

Check your answers with the error key on page 101.

VERBS—MODALS

1. After all modals use the simple form of the verb (V). The following
is a list of modals:

can	could	must
may	should	will
might	would	shall

MODAL + V
They *can walk* five miles without getting tired.

MODAL + V
They *could walk* five miles without getting tired.

2. Use the past participle after the modal + *have*.

MODAL + HAVE + PAST PART.
Mr. and·Mrs. Smith *might have enjoyed* the party.

MODAL + HAVE + PAST PART.
He *should have sent* in his application earlier.

MODAL + HAVE + PAST PART.
We *should* not *have eaten* such a big dinner.

3. When you change direct speech to indirect speech, *could*, *would*,
should, and *might* do not change form.

DIRECT	INDIRECT
"You *should* always *do* your homework."	The teacher said that I *should* always *do* my homework.
"I *might ask* her out."	He said that he *might ask* her out.

4. Use *must have* + past participle for past conclusion only.

The ground is wet; it *must have* rained.   (conclusion)

5. Use *had* + infinitive for past obligation.

I *had to go* to the dentist yesterday.   (obligation)

ERROR EXAMPLES

A. WRONG: Beth must to take the bus yesterday because her car was being repaired.
   RIGHT: Beth *had to take* the bus yesterday because her car was being repaired.

B. WRONG: We must to water our plants regularly.
   RIGHT: We must *water* our plants regularly.

C. WRONG: They could walked to school because it was close.
   RIGHT: They could *walk* to school because it was close.

D. WRONG: The show will have begin by the time we arrive.
   RIGHT: The show will have *begun* by the time we arrive.

E. WRONG: John said that he might have gone to Harvard next year.
   RIGHT: John said that he might *go* to Harvard next year.

EXERCISE: Put "C" if the sentence is correct. Put "X" if there is an error in the modals.

_____1.   My brother has to walk ten miles to buy some gas last weekend.

_____2.   There is no one outside the theater; the performance must have been cancelled.

_____3.   They must to sign up for that class by this Friday.

_____4.   We would have went to Florida, but it was having an unusual cold spell.

_____5.   Mrs. Jones told me that she might have baked a cake for my birthday tomorrow if she has time.

_____6.   Susan said she might leave before dinner.

_____7.   They might go to the store a few minutes ago.

_____8. When my baby got very ill, I must have called the doctor immediately.

_____9. The boys should not had made so much noise.

_____10. I will be very happy when I graduate this year.

Check your answers with the error key on page 102.

VERBS—VERBALS

1. The following verbs can be followed by the infinitive (*to* + V) as the direct object:

agree	forbid	mean
care	forget	offer
decide	hope	plan
deserve	intend	pretend
fail	learn	refuse

TO + V
Mr. Smith and Mr. Parker deserve *to be* promoted.

TO + V
They decided *to leave* early.

TO + V
The secretary offered *to come* in early.

TO + V
He hopes *to see* them again.

2. The following verbs can be followed by the gerund (V + *ing*) as the direct object:

admit	deny	postpone
appreciate	enjoy	practice
avoid	finish	stop
cannot help	keep	suggest
consider		

V + ING
She enjoyed *meeting* them.

V + ING
I have never considered *quitting* my job.

V + ING
He finishes *studying* every evening at ten.

V + ING
He admitted *committing* the crime.

3. The following verb phrases (verb + preposition) can be followed by the gerund (V + *ing*). Remember that gerunds, not infinitives, follow prepositions in general and not just the prepositions in this list. See also *Style—Prepositions in Combinations*, page 198.

be accustomed to	decide on	plan on
be interested in	get through	put off
be opposed to	keep on	think about
be used to	look forward to	think of

PREP. + V + ING
She was not used *to living* in a dormitory.

PREP. + V + ING
He kept *on driving* even though he was tired.

PREP. + V + ING
He has been looking forward *to meeting* you.

4. a) Use the simple form of the verb (V) after the causative verbs *let*, *make*, and *have* when the second verb is active.

V
He made the children *look* both ways before crossing the street.

V
The teacher let him *leave* early.

V
The teacher had had the class *begin* to write a composition when the bell rang.

b) Use a past participle after the causative verbs *have* and *get* when the second verb is passive in meaning.

PAST PART.
She had her passport *stamped* at the immigration office.

PAST PART.
They got their house *painted* last summer.

5. The following verbs of perception are followed by the simple form of the verb (V) *or* the present participle (V + *ing*):

feel	see
hear	smell
notice	watch
observe	

I heard the baby	OR	I heard the baby
V		V + ING
cry.		*crying*.

Jane observed him	OR	Jane observed him
V		V + ING
leave.		*leaving*.

ERROR EXAMPLES

A. WRONG: The professor forbids the students leaving early.
    RIGHT: The professor forbids the students *to leave* early.

B. WRONG: She could not help to laugh at his foolishness.
    RIGHT: She could not help *laughing* at his foolishness.

C. WRONG: I am opposed to go to war.
    RIGHT: I am opposed to *going* to war.

D. WRONG: Do not let those children to eat a lot of candy.
    RIGHT: Do not let those children *eat* a lot of candy.

E. WRONG: I was surprised to see a person to cry at that movie.
    RIGHT: I was surprised to see a person *cry* at that movie.

                              OR

             I was surprised to see a person *crying* at that movie.

F. WRONG: She had her phone hook up when she returned from abroad.
    RIGHT: She had her phone *hooked up* when she returned from abroad.

G. WRONG: He had his annual chest X-ray taking yesterday.
    RIGHT: He had his annual chest X-ray *taken* yesterday.

EXERCISE: Put "C" if the sentence is correct. Put "X" if there is an error with the verbal (infinitive, gerund, simple verb, or participle) that follows the main verb.

_____1. Blocks from the stadium, we could hear the people to cheer.

_____2. Do you think you might enjoy living in a small town?

_____3. I always make the children to pick up their toys.

_____4. The official offered to help me get my papers in order.

_____5. I had the paperboy stop delivering papers for the month of July.

_____6. Since you need more money, you should not stop to try to find a better job.

_____7. He was not used to making decisions by himself.

_____8. Jane had her blood pressure taking recently.

_____9. What made the student decide leaving early?

_____10. I am looking forward to see you again soon.

_____11. What do you think of our having a party to celebrate?

_____12. She had her shoes dyed to match her dress.

_____13. She could not help noticing the man to cry.

_____14. One should avoid eating a heavy meal late in the evening.

_____15. We had Tom to make the dinner reservations.

_____16. Since he promised to take care of it, his parents let the boy to buy a dog.

_____17. He was not used to living alone.

_____18. Bob had his gas and electricity turn on when he moved into his new apartment last week.

_____19. When will you get through to read that book?

_____20. The doctor had Mrs. Jones take ten pills a day for her heart.

_____21. Their boss never has them to stay past 5:00 P.M.

_____22. They saw the thief running from the bank.

_____23. The professor had us to read the first half of the book by Monday.

_____24. Please do not fail registering before the deadline.

_____25. As I entered the house, I smelled the food cooking.

_____26. We had our university identification pictures taken yesterday.

_____27. The law of that country forbids anyone under eighteen driving a car.

_____28. The teacher made us using our imaginations.

_____29. The class could not help to laugh when the teacher dropped all his papers.

_____30. When we decided to stay in Mexico longer, we had our visas renewed.

Check your answers with the error key on page 103.

VERBS—PAST PARTICIPLES

The past participle is used in the following:

1. *Present Perfect*

> PAST PART.
> He has *broken* the world's track record.

2. *Past Perfect*

> PAST PART.
> Mary had *spoken* to John about the matter before I arrived.

3. *Unreal Past Conditional*

> PAST PART.   PAST PART.
> If he had *been* here on time, he would have *heard* the news.

4. *Passive*

> PAST PART.
> The president's re-election was *taken* for granted by his constituents.

5. *Perfect Infinitive*

PAST PART.

I would like to have *grown* up on a farm.

6. *Perfect Participle*

PAST PART.

Having *swum* ten laps in the Olympic pool, he was exhausted.

7. *Adjective*

PAST PART.

The *stolen* watch was a very expensive piece of jewelry.

8. *Past Modal*

PAST PART.

Molly said that I should not have *gone* to that movie.

9. *Introductory Verbal Phrase*

PAST PART.

Seen from a distance, the house appeared to be in good condition.

NOTE:

The following are some of the verbs in English whose past participle forms (with the exception of *hurt* and *hear*) are *different from the past tense forms.*

Verb	Past Participle	Verb	Past Participle	Verb	Past Participle
be	been	give	given	show	shown
begin	begun	go	gone	sing	sung
break	broken	grow	grown	speak	spoken
choose	chosen	hear	heard	steal	stolen
do	done	hurt	hurt	swim	swum
drink	drunk	know	known	take	taken
drive	driven	ride	ridden	tear	torn
eat	eaten	ring	rung	throw	thrown
fly	flown	run	run	wear	worn
forgive	forgiven	see	seen	write	written

ERROR EXAMPLES

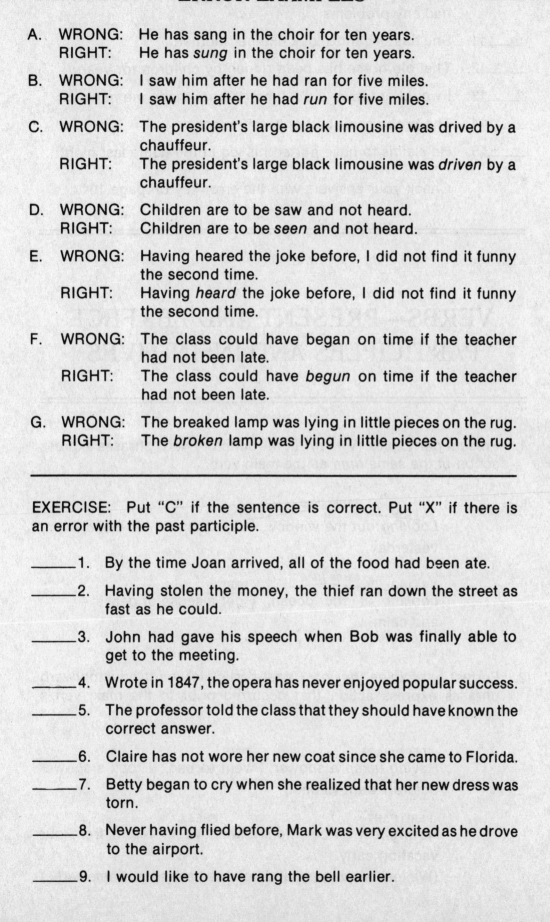

A. WRONG: He has sang in the choir for ten years.
    RIGHT: He has *sung* in the choir for ten years.

B. WRONG: I saw him after he had ran for five miles.
    RIGHT: I saw him after he had *run* for five miles.

C. WRONG: The president's large black limousine was drived by a
             chauffeur.
    RIGHT: The president's large black limousine was *driven* by a
             chauffeur.

D. WRONG: Children are to be saw and not heard.
    RIGHT: Children are to be *seen* and not heard.

E. WRONG: Having heared the joke before, I did not find it funny
             the second time.
    RIGHT: Having *heard* the joke before, I did not find it funny
             the second time.

F. WRONG: The class could have began on time if the teacher
             had not been late.
    RIGHT: The class could have *begun* on time if the teacher
             had not been late.

G. WRONG: The breaked lamp was lying in little pieces on the rug.
    RIGHT: The *broken* lamp was lying in little pieces on the rug.

EXERCISE: Put "C" if the sentence is correct. Put "X" if there is
an error with the past participle.

_____1. By the time Joan arrived, all of the food had been ate.

_____2. Having stolen the money, the thief ran down the street as
           fast as he could.

_____3. John had gave his speech when Bob was finally able to
           get to the meeting.

_____4. Wrote in 1847, the opera has never enjoyed popular success.

_____5. The professor told the class that they should have known the
           correct answer.

_____6. Claire has not wore her new coat since she came to Florida.

_____7. Betty began to cry when she realized that her new dress was
           torn.

_____8. Never having flied before, Mark was very excited as he drove
           to the airport.

_____9. I would like to have rang the bell earlier.

_____10. If he had shown the official his passport, he would not have had any problems.

_____11. She has began to look like her mother.

_____12. That old horse has been ridden by children for years.

_____13. I would not have did it if he had not made me nervous.

_____14. The broke chair had only three legs.

_____15. He claims to have hurted his leg in the game last night.

Check your answers with the error key on page 104.

VERBS—PRESENT AND PERFECT PARTICIPLES AND INFINITIVES

1. Present participles (V + *ing*) in introductory verb phrases express action of the *same time* as the main verb.

V + ING _____ *same time* _____ PAST
Looking out the window, I *saw* John on his bicycle yesterday.

V + ING _____ *same time* _____ PRES.
Looking at the ocean, I *get* a sense of peace and calm.

2. Perfect participles (*having* + past participle) in introductory verb phrases express action that occurred prior to the main verb's action.

PERF. PART. _____ PAST
Having taken a shower, I went to bed. (I took a shower *before* I went to bed.)

PERF. PART. _____ PRES.
Having lost all our money, we *have* to return from our vacation early.
(We lost our money, and now we have to go home early.)

3. The present infinitive (*to* + V) expresses action that occurs at the same time as or future to the main verb.

<pre>
                      PRES.
             PRES.   INFIN.
</pre>
I *hope to pass* the test tomorrow.   (*To pass* is future to *hope*.)

<pre>
                      PRES.
             PAST   INFIN.
</pre>
I *wanted to leave* early yesterday. (*To leave* is same time as or future to *wanted*.)

4. The perfect infinitive (*to* + *have* + past participle) expresses action that occurred prior to the main verb's action.

<pre>
        PRES.   PERF. INFIN.
</pre>
I *hope to have passed* the test I took yesterday.

(I hope now that I passed the test I took yesterday.)

<pre>
             PRES.   PERF. INFIN.
</pre>
He *is reported to have died* yesterday.

(He apparently died yesterday and now his death is being reported.)

<pre>
             PAST   PERF. INFIN.
</pre>
He *was reported to have died* the day before.

(He apparently died the day before his death was reported.)

<pre>
             PRES.   PERF. INFIN.
</pre>
I *would like to have lived* in the seventeenth century.

(I wish now that I had lived at some time in the past.)

ERROR EXAMPLES

A. WRONG: Getting a driver's license, Paul was able to drive from Boston to Los Angeles.

RIGHT: *Having gotten* a driver's license, Paul was able to drive from Boston to Los Angeles.

B. WRONG: When I saw you yesterday, I would have liked to have stopped and talked·to you.

RIGHT: When I saw you yesterday, I would have liked to *stop* and *talk* to you.

C. WRONG: She is reputed to be a spy during World War II.

RIGHT: She is reputed *to have been* a spy during World War II.

D.   WRONG: He is said to having written a great novel.
     RIGHT: He is said *to have written* a great novel.

EXERCISE: Put "C" if the sentence is correct. Put "X" if there is an error in the participle or the infinitive.

_____1.   They chose not to have attended the meeting.

_____2.   She would have liked to study abroad.

_____3.   The notorious criminal is reported to having surrendered yesterday.

_____4.   Applying at the University of Arizona, she anxiously awaited her acceptance.

_____5.   They are presumed to die in the crash last weekend.

_____6.   Having studied diligently, he found the examination quite easy.

_____7.   Writing the letter, she mailed it on her way to work.

_____8.   The police officer wanted to give me a ride home.

_____9.   Catching several fish, they cooked them for dinner.

_____10. Betty should have remembered to call me last night.

Check your answers with the error key on page 104.

CHAPTER QUIZ—Verbs

DIRECTIONS· Put "C" if the sentence is correct.
Put "X" if there is an error in the verb.

_____1. Mr. and Mrs. Jones stopped smoking a year ago and have not started again.

_____2. After jogging, I was so hungry that I could have ate a horse.

_____3. Many people who were opposed to use nuclear energy in any form demonstrated against the opening of the new nuclear power plant.

_____4. The license bureau demands that a person renew his license before it expires.

_____5. For several years now, the student body is attempting to gain more influence over university policies.

_____6. If I will get the money in time, I will go to California on my next vacation.

_____7. After agreeing to make the necessary changes in the contract, Mr. Martin had his secretary type the amended version for us to sign.

_____8. Much to his surprise, when Robert arrived in London, he had found several relatives waiting for him at the airport.

_____9. Reading several books on that subject, Bill considered himself an expert.

_____10. Ralph wishes that he went to the bank this morning before he went to work.

DIRECTIONS: In the space provided, put the letter of the word or phrase that *best completes* the sentence.

_____1. They told me that I _____ the tap water in that country.

(A) must not have drank
(B) could not drunk
(C) should not have drunk
(D) could have drink

_____2. The doctor was very surprised that his patient had let his condition _____ so much before calling him.

(A) deteriorate
(B) to deteriorate
(C) to deteriorating
(D) deteriorating

_____3. If he had applied by August 15, the university_____
him this semester.

(A) would accepted
(B) had accepted
(C) should have accept
(D) would have accepted

_____4. When we finally bought stock in that company, the market
_____ its peak and the stock was declining in
value.

(A) did already reach
(B) has already reached
(C) was already reached
(D) had already reached

_____5. They are said _____ a dynamic new play.

(A) to have wrote
(B) to have written
(C) to have writing
(D) have written

_____6. Last year in the middle of the most severe drought in
recent history, the already dwindling tribe finally _____
_____ to leave its ancestral land and to look for a new
place to live.

(A) had decided
(B) decided
(C) has decided
(D) decides

_____7. It was important that they _____ before the
curtain went up last night.

(A) arrive
(B) have arrived
(C) arrived
(D) had arrived

_____8. I could see Susan's hands _____ slightly as she
placed her papers on the podium and prepared to address
the audience.

(A) to tremble
(B) trembles
(C) trembled
(D) trembling

_____9. The babysitter agreed _____ the children before putting them to bed.

(A) for bathing
(B) to bath
(C) to bathe
(D) to giving a bath

_____10. When the famous pianist was a child, he was accustomed to _____ for several hours a day.

(A) practice
(B) practicing
(C) practiced
(D) be practicing

Check your answers with the error key on page 105.

ERROR KEYS

VERBS—Tense

ERROR KEY

<u>X</u> 1. (I *was* in Mexico). See rule 2.

<u>C</u> 2.

<u>X</u> 3. (He *was* a student). See rule 2.

<u>C</u> 4.

<u>X</u> 5. (and *went* to lunch). See rule 2.

<u>C</u> 6.

<u>X</u> 7. (they *recognized* us). See rule 2.

<u>C</u> 8.

<u>X</u> 9. (*has seen* ten patients). See rule 1.

<u>X</u> 10. (He *has studied* English). See rule 1.

VERBS—Time Clauses

ERROR KEY

<u>X</u> 1. (when it *is* spring)

<u>X</u> 2. (when winter *comes*)

<u>C</u> 3.

<u>X</u> 4. (the children *visit* their grandmother)

<u>C</u> 5.

<u>X</u> 6. (when you *are* in Scotland)

<u>X</u> 7. (critics *see*)

<u>C</u> 8.

<u>C</u> 9.

<u>X</u> 10. (Joan *gets*)

VERBS—Verbs of "Demand"

ERROR KEY

__X__ 1. (employees *take*)

__C__ 2.

__X__ 3. (that I *stop* smoking)

__C__ 4.

__X__ 5. (that John *have*)

__X__ 6. (that his crew *have*)

__C__ 7.

__X__ 8. (that Mr. Smith *not leave*) See note.

__C__ 9.

__X__ 10. (that a driver *renew*)

VERBS—Wishes

ERROR KEY

__C__ 1.

__X__ 2. (he *did not* have to). See rule 1.

__X__ 3. (he *had not* lost). See rule 3.

__C__ 4.

__X__ 5. (that he *had*). See rule 1.

__X__ 6. (he *had not ignored*). See rule 3.

__X__ 7. (that I *were* earning). See rule 2.

__X__ 8. (father *did*). See rule 1.

__C__ 9.

__X__ 10. (she *were* still living). See rule 2.

VERBS—Conditionals

ERROR KEY

__X__ 1. (he would not *have broken*) See rule 2b. See also *Verbs—Past Participles*, page 82.

___X___ 2.   (If he *were* taller). See rule 2a and note b.

___X___ 3.   (If my apartment *were* larger). See rule 2a and note b.

___X___ 4.   (If he *were* ready). See rule 2a and note b.

___X___ 5.   (I *would have gone*). See rule 2b.

___X___ 6.   (If Betty *had driven*). See rule 2b and note a.

___X___ 7.   (If *I finish*). See rule 1.

___C___ 8.

___X___ 9.   (he *would* not have lost). See rule 2b.

___X___ 10. (I would have *seen* him). See rule 2b. See also *Verbs— Past Participles*, page 91.

___C___ 11.

___X___ 12. (If *you take*). See rule 1.

___X___ 13. (he *would* certainly *have bought*). See rule 2b.

___C___ 14.

___X___ 15. (I *would have paid*). See rule 2b.

VERBS—Modals

ERROR KEY

___X___ 1.   (*had* to walk). See rule 5.

___C___ 2.

___X___ 3.   (must *sign up*). See rule 1.

___X___ 4.   (would have *gone*). See rule 2. See also *Verbs—Past Participles*, page 91.

___X___ 5.   (might *bake*). See rule 3.

___C___ 6.

___X___ 7.   (might *have gone*). See rule 2.

___X___ 8.   (I *had to call*). See rule 4.

___X___ 9.   (should not *have* made). See rule 1.

___C___ 10.

VERBS—Verbals

ERROR KEY

_X_ 1. (hear the people *cheer*) OR (hear the people *cheering*). See rule 5.

_C_ 2.

_X_ 3. (make the children *pick up*). See rule 4a.

_C_ 4.

_C_ 5.

_X_ 6. (stop *trying* to find). See rule 2.

_C_ 7.

_X_ 8. (pressure *taken* recently). See rule 4b.

_X_ 9. (decide *to leave* early). See rule 1.

_X_ 10. (looking forward to *seeing*). See rule 3.

_C_ 11.

_C_ 12.

_X_ 13. (noticing the man *cry*) OR (noticing the man *crying*). See rule 5.

_C_ 14.

_X_ 15. (Tom *make* the dinner). See rule 4a.

_X_ 16. (let the boy *buy*). See rule 4a.

_C_ 17.

_X_ 18. (electricity *turned on* when). See rule 4b.

_X_ 19. (get through *reading*). See rule 3.

_C_ 20.

_X_ 21. (has them *stay*). See rule 4a.

_C_ 22.

_X_ 23. (had us *read* the first). See rule 4a.

_X_ 24. (do not fail *to register*). See rule 1.

_C_ 25.

_C_ 26.

_X_ 27. (forbids anyone under eighteen *to drive*). See rule 1.

_X_ 28. (made us *use* our). See rule 4a.

_X_ 29. (could not help *laughing*). See rule 2.

_C_ 30.

VERBS—Past Participles

ERROR KEY

__X__ 1.   (had been *eaten*). See rule 4 and note.

__C__ 2.

__X__ 3.   (had *given* his speech). See rule 2 and note.

__X__ 4.   (*Written* in 1847). See rule 9 and note.

__C__ 5.

__X__ 6.   (has not *worn*). See rule 1 and note.

__C__ 7.

__X__ 8.   (Never having *flown*). See rule 6 and note.

__X__ 9.   (to have *rung*). See rule 5 and note.

__C__ 10.

__X__ 11.   (She has *begun*). See rule 1 and note.

__C__ 12.

__X__ 13.   (would not have *done*). See rule 3 and note.

__X__ 14.   (*broken* chair). See rule 7 and note.

__X__ 15.   (to have *hurt*). See rule 5 and note.

VERBS—Present and Perfect Participles and Infinitives

ERROR KEY

__X__ 1.   (chose not *to attend*). See rule 3.

__C__ 2.

__X__ 3.   (to *have* surrendered). See rule 4.

__X__ 4.   (*Having applied*). See rule 2.

__X__ 5.   (to *have died*). See rule 4.

__C__ 6.

__X__ 7.   (*Having written*). See rule 2.

__C__ 8.

__X__ 9.   (*Having caught*). See rule 2.

__C__ 10.

CHAPTER QUIZ—Verbs

ERROR KEY

___C___ 1.

___X___ 2. (could have *eaten*). See *Past Participles*, page 91.

___X___ 3. (opposed to *using*). See *Verbals*, page 87.

___C___ 4.

___X___ 5. (*has been* attempting). See *Tense*, page 75.

___X___ 6. (If I *get*). See *Conditionals*, page 82.

___C___ 7.

___X___ 8. (he *found*). See *Tense*, page 75.

___X___ 9. (*Having read*). See *Present and Perfect Participles* and *Infinitives*, page 94.

___X___ 10. (that he *had gone*). See *Wishes*, page 80.

___C___ 1. (A) See *Modals*, page 85.
    (B) Same as A
    (C) Correct
    (D) Same as A

___A___ 2. (A) Correct
    (B) See *Verbals*, page 87.
    (C) Same as B
    (D) Same as B

___D___ 3. (A) See *Conditionals*, page 82.
    (B) Same as A
    (C) Same as A
    (D) Correct

___D___ 4. (A) See *Tense*, page 75.
    (B) Same as A
    (C) Same as A
    (D) Correct

___B___ 5. (A) See *Present and Perfect Participles* and *Infinitives*, page 94.
    (B) Correct
    (C) Same as A
    (D) Same as A

___B___ 6. (A) See *Tense*, page 75.
        (B) Correct
        (C) Same as A
        (D) Same as A

___A___ 7. (A) Correct
        (B) See *Verbs of "Demand,"* page 78.
        (C) Same as B
        (D) Same as B

___D___ 8. (A) See *Verbals*, page 87.
        (B) Same as A
        (C) Same as A
        (D) Correct

___C___ 9. (A) See *Verbals*, page 87.
        (B) Same as A
        (C) Correct
        (D) Same as A

___B___ 10. (A) See *Verbals*, page 87.
        (B) Correct
        (C) Same as A
        (D) Same as A

X

PRONOUNS

PRONOUNS—RELATIVES

Who, whom, which, that, and whose are relative pronouns used to introduce relative clauses (adjective clauses). For the who/whom problem, see page 111.

1. Who and whom are used for persons.

> I saw the man who is famous for inventing plastic.
>
> Give it to the man whom you already know.

2. Which is used for things.

> Is this the 104 bus, which goes to the Southgate Shopping Center?

3. That can be used for persons or things.

> Here is the man that can answer your questions.
>
> Did you find the book that you were looking for?

4. Whose is used to show possession. It can be followed by persons or things.

> This is the man whose car was towed away.
>
> Do you know the doctor whose children I teach?

ERROR EXAMPLES

A.   WRONG: He is the student which always arrives late.
       RIGHT: He is the student *who* always arrives late.

OR

He is the student *that* always arrives late.

B.   WRONG: Saudi Arabia is a country who exports oil all over the world.
       RIGHT: Saudi Arabia is a country *which* exports oil all over the world.

OR

Saudi Arabia is a country *that* exports oil all over the world.

C.   WRONG: We visited the building what is famous for its unusual design.
       RIGHT: We visited the building *which* is famous for its unusual design.

OR

We visited the building *that* is famous for its unusual design.

D.   WRONG: There was a story in the paper about the man that his car was stolen.
       RIGHT: There was a story in the paper about the man *whose* car was stolen.

EXERCISE: Put "C" if the sentence is correct. Put "X" if there is an error in the relative pronoun.

_____1.   I like novels who deal with philosophical questions.

_____2.   The company did not want to hire a man that his experience was so limited.

_____3.   The family whose house burned down was on television.

_____4.   She wore a dress what everyone considered extravagant.

_____5.   Where can one catch the train which goes to Flower Square?

_____6.   The ship that we boarded in Rio was bound for Marseilles.

_____7.   John did not want to do business with a man which had been in prison.

_____8.   Take your car back to the man who sold it to you.

_____9. That is the baby which has been in the incubator for three months.

_____10. The woman that her photograph was in the paper is making a speech at the town hall tonight.

Check your answers with the error key on page 127.

PRONOUNS—PERSONAL—CASE

1. Subject pronouns (*I*, *you*, *he*, *she*, *it*, *we*, and *they*) are used in the subject position and after the verb *to be*.

> S
> *They* arrived safely last night.

> BE + S PRON.
> It *was they* who knocked on the door last night.

2. Object pronouns (*me*, *you*, *him*, *her*, *it*, *us*, and *them*) are used as objects of verbs and prepositions and as subjects of infinitives.

> VERB OBJ.
> I *told him* the news.

> PREP.   OBJ.
> *Between you and me*, the economic situation looks bad.

> S   INFIN.
> We asked *him to bring* a salad to the party.

NOTES:

a. Pronouns in apposition* are in the same case as the pronouns they follow. Example: Let's (Let us), *you and me*, go dancing Friday night. *Us* is the object of *let*. *You* and *me* must also be in the objective case.

b. Pronouns after the conjunctions *as* or *than* should be subject pronouns when they function as subjects.

> S
> He is as tall as *I* (am tall).

S

John plays soccer as well as *he* (plays soccer).

S

They are more diligent students than *we* (are).

c. The correct forms of the reflexive pronouns for *him* and *them* are *himself* and *themselves*, NOT *hisself* or *theirselves*.

*An *appositive* is a noun or pronoun that follows another noun or pronoun and identifies the first noun or pronoun.

ERROR EXAMPLES

A. WRONG: Jane and him planned to go to the movies.
    RIGHT: Jane and *he* planned to go to the movies.

B. WRONG: She sold the car to Mary and he.
    RIGHT: She sold the car to Mary and *him*.

C. WRONG: I never met a man as kind as him.
    RIGHT: I never met a man as kind as *he*.

D. WRONG: For you and I arriving on time will be difficult.
    RIGHT: For you and *me* arriving on time will be difficult.

E. WRONG: He specifically told them, Bob and he, to get ready.
    RIGHT: He specifically told them, Bob and *him*, to get ready.

F. WRONG: Several times during the semester the teacher asked he to speak to the class.
    RIGHT: Several times during the semester the teacher asked *him* to speak to the class.

G. WRONG: Ask him to do it hisself.
    RIGHT: Ask him to do it *himself*.

F. WRONG: They do not want to go by theirselves.
    RIGHT: They do not want to go by *themselves*.

EXERCISE: Put "C" if the sentence is correct. Put "X" if there is an error in pronoun case.

_____1. I was surprised to learn that Betty and him were hurt in the accident.

_____2. I often remember when Paul and I visited Rome.

_____3. He moved the furniture by hisself.

_____4. She gave us, Margaret and I, the notes we missed in class.

_____5. They were sitting by themselves next to the swimming pool.

_____6. That project is the responsibility of Susan and she.

_____7. Let us keep this secret between you and me.

_____8. Do not forget to give the message to Bob and me.

_____9. The tourists asked us, my cousin and me, how to get to the museum.

_____10. Please be sure to notify my husband or I when the package arrives.

_____11. The children assembled the toy house by theirselves.

_____12. How often do you have the opportunity to meet a man as intelligent as him?

_____13. For the majority of us the issue is rather confusing.

_____14. Mary will never be as rich as I.

_____15. It is her, the one whom nobody likes.

Check your answers with the error key on page 127.

PRONOUNS—*WHO/WHOM*

Who and *whoever* are subject pronouns
Whom and *whomever* are object pronouns.

1. In general, the patterns for *who* and *whoever* are:

a) *who (whoever)* + verb

S
WHO + VERB
The woman *who sang* yesterday has studied voice for years.

S
WHO + VERB
Who came to the party?

S
WHOEVER + VERB

Give the money to *whoever needs* it.

S
WHOEVER + VERB

I said that *whoever had finished* could leave.

b)   *whom (whomever)* + subject + verb

OBJ.
WHOM + S + VERB

The woman *whom I met* yesterday is a voice teacher.

OBJ.
WHOMEVER + S + VERB

Give it to *whomever you like.*

2.   Sometimes expressions like the following separate *who (whoever)* or *whom (whomever)* from its own verb or subject and verb:

"I think"
"she said"
"we know"
"do you know"

S
WHO ⌒ VERB

He is a student *who* <u>*we believe*</u> *can do* the job.

S
WHO ⌒ VERB

Give the job to the person *who* <u>*you think*</u> *is* best suited for it.

OBJ.
WHOM ⌒ S + VERB

He is a man *whom* <u>*I feel*</u> *you can trust.*

S
WHOEVER ⌒ VERB

Tell the story to *whoever* <u>*you think*</u> *should hear* it.

ERROR EXAMPLES

A.   WRONG: I saw the man who John spoke to.
    RIGHT: I saw the man *whom* John spoke to.

B.   WRONG: Do not speak to people whom are strangers.
    RIGHT: Do not speak to people *who* are strangers.

C. WRONG: Take your problem to the person whom you think can help you.
    RIGHT: Take your problem to the person *who* you think can help you.

D. WRONG: She gave it to the only person who she believed.
    RIGHT: She gave it to the only person *whom* she believed.

E. WRONG: They will award the prize to whomever is best.
    RIGHT: They will award the prize to *whoever* is best.

F. WRONG: They chose whomever was most interested.
    RIGHT: They chose *whoever* was most interested.

EXERCISE: Put "C" if the sentence is correct. Put "X" if there is a *who/whom* error.

_____1. I met the new people whom I thought were from your country.

_____2. You should ask advice from people who you trust.

_____3. Ask whoever is willing to come early.

_____4. There is the new director who I think you met before.

_____5. The man who you think is a doctor is actually a male nurse.

_____6. She was the person who the teacher chose to speak at the final ceremony.

_____7. It is pleasant to be with people who like us and whom we like.

_____8. Ask anyone who you think is interested to join the team.

_____9. Whom do you think will be ready on time?

_____10. Take this to whomever the supervisor chose to do the job.

_____11. The lawyer whom handled that case disappeared.

_____12. Assign this project to whoever you like.

_____13. Deliver this envelope to whomever answers the door.

_____14. It was Jack and I who he thought were at fault in the situation.

_____15. Many women whom are working would prefer to be at home.

Check your answers with the error key on page 128.

PRONOUNS—POSSESSIVES

Use the possessive case* with gerunds (V + *ing* used as a noun).

POSSESSIVE   V + ING
I resented *their interrupting* our conversations.

POSSESSIVE V + ING
His swimming is getting a lot better.

POSS.   V + ING
Because of *your leaving* late, you will have to take a taxi in order to catch your train.

*Remember that the possessive pronouns are *my*, *your*, *his*, *her*, *its*, *our*, *their*, and *one's*.

NOTE:

It's is *not* a possessive pronoun but a contraction of *it is*.

ERROR EXAMPLES

A. WRONG: Susan did not like him making a lot of noise while she was studying.
    RIGHT: Susan did not like *his* making a lot of noise while she was studying.

B. WRONG: Betty cannot remember you telling her that story.
    RIGHT: Betty cannot remember *your* telling her that story.

C. WRONG: They did not like him calling so late at night.
    RIGHT: They did not like *his* calling so late at night.

D. WRONG: I approve of one living on his own before marriage.
    RIGHT: I approve of *one's* living on his own before marriage.

E. WRONG: I could not sleep last night because of them shouting next door.
    RIGHT: I could not sleep last night because of *their* shouting next door.

F. WRONG: The chairman congratulated us on us winning the contest.
    RIGHT: The chairman congratulated us on *our* winning the contest.

G. WRONG: When we had a dog, I can remember it chasing birds.
    RIGHT: When we had a dog, I can remember *its* chasing birds.

H. WRONG: Professor Jones was angry at me coming late to class every day.
    RIGHT: Professor Jones was angry at *my* coming late to class every day.

EXERCISE: Put "C" if the sentence is correct. Put "X" if there is an error with the possessive pronoun.

_____1. Our neighbors complained about our playing the stereo too loudly.

_____2. I sadly thought of you saying good-bye.

_____3. Were you surprised at their buying a new car?

_____4. I cannot imagine his refusing that job.

_____5. What did you think of them leaving so abruptly?

_____6. My neighbor has a lovely cat, but it meowing bothers me at night.

_____7. Him playing the drums day and night made his roommates very angry.

_____8. Her winning first prize delighted us a great deal.

_____9. I really appreciate your trying to arrive on time.

_____10. Mrs. Allen was concerned about me having to drive so far every day.

_____11. Your telling him that might disturb him a great deal.

_____12. His family was elated when they heard of him winning the race.

_____13. Mr. Smith was upset by their fast driving.

_____14. Did the teacher mind us whispering in the back of the room?

_____15. My boss finally approved of me taking my vacation in August.

Check your answers with the error key on page 128.

PRONOUNS—FAULTY REFERENCE

The antecedent* of a pronoun must be *clearly* understood.

> ANTECEDENT   PRON.
> When *Betty* was in college, *she* wrote to her family every week. (*She* clearly refers to *Betty*.)

> ANTECEDENT   PRON.
> As *Bob* got off the plane, *he* waved to his father.
> (*He* clearly refers to *Bob*.)

> ANTECEDENT   PRON.
> As Don explained his *theory* to me, I found *it* fascinating.
> (*It* clearly refers to *theory*.)

*An *antecedent* is the noun or pronoun a pronoun refers to.

ERROR EXAMPLES

A. WRONG: Mary told Paula that she had to read Plato's *Republic*.
                    (*She* can refer to *Mary* or *Paula*.)
     RIGHT: Mary told Paula, "I have to read Plato's *Republic*."

B. WRONG: Paul saw his friend as he was walking across the campus.
                    (*He* can refer to *Paul* or *his friend*.)
     RIGHT: While Paul was walking across the campus, he saw his friend.

C. WRONG: Sylvia and Mary saw a movie yesterday, and she said it was wonderful.
                    (*She* can refer to *Sylvia* or *Mary*.)
     RIGHT: Sylvia and Mary saw a movie yesterday, and Sylvia said it was wonderful.

D. WRONG: I put the vase on the glass table and it broke.
                    (*It* can refer to *vase* or *table*.)
     RIGHT: The vase broke as I put it on the glass table.

E. WRONG: In the book it says to cook the meat for several hours.
                    (*It* has *no* antecedent in this context.)
     RIGHT: *The book* says to cook the meat for several hours.

EXERCISE: Put "C" if the sentence is correct. Put "X" if the pronoun does not clearly refer to one antecedent or if it has no antecedent.

_____1.   Mr. Smith told Mr. Jones that he had lost a lot of money in the stock market.

_____2.   In the telephone directory, it says to call directory assistance in that situation.

_____3.   When Peter finished the examination, he gave it to the professor.

_____4.   Cathy saw her friend as she was driving home from work.

_____5.   When John put a new frame on the picture, it looked strange.

_____6.   The laundry was not dry enough for Susan to bring it into the house.

_____7.   He put all his savings in the stock market, and it suffered great losses that year.

_____8.   When Jack was in the navy, he learned electronics.

_____9.   In the newspaper it says there is renewed interest in the silver market.

_____10. The A Team played the B Team yesterday, and now it is in first place.

Check your answers with the error key on page 129.

PRONOUNS—PERSON

Do not carelessly change the person of a pronoun.

PRON.
A *student* has to expect to work hard when *he* goes to college.

OR

A student has to expect to work hard when *she* goes to college.

PRON.

One should brush *one's* teeth twice daily.

OR

One should brush *his* teeth twice daily.

NOTES:

a. A *student*, a *person*, or *one* can use the following third-person-singular pronouns: *he*, *she*, or *he or she*; *him*, *her*, or *him or her*; and *his*, *her*, or *his or her*.

A student must renew *his or her* library card every year.

b. The possessive pronoun for *one* can be *one's* or *his* (see also note a) but never *ones*.

ERROR EXAMPLES

A. WRONG: A person can expect to receive a traffic ticket when we drive too fast.

RIGHT: A person can expect to receive a traffic ticket when *he* drives too fast.

B. WRONG: When one has a toothache, you should go to the dentist.

RIGHT: When one has a toothache, *one* should go to the dentist.

C. WRONG: One should remember to pay your telephone bill on time.

RIGHT: One should remember to pay *one's* telephone bill on time.

D. WRONG: One should have ones teeth checked regularly.

RIGHT: One should have *one's* teeth checked regularly.

EXERCISE: Put "C" if the sentence is correct. Put "X" if there is an error with the person of the pronoun.

_____1. When a person eats well, you feel well.

_____2. For successful completion of this exercise, one must give his complete attention to the task at hand.

_____3. One should always pay your rent promptly.

_____4. One should never forget his obligations to his family.

_____5. One often forgets one's early failures.

_____6. When a person is learning to play a musical instrument, we must practice several hours a day.

_____7. When one goes through life, we meet many challenges.

_____8. One can always rely on one's friends in time of need.

_____9. When a person goes to a foreign country, he must expect many things to be different.

_____10. When you find yourself in an air-conditioned theater, one often wishes he had a sweater.

Check your answers with the error key on page 130.

PRONOUNS—NUMBER*

1. Pronouns must agree in number with their *antecedents* (the noun or pronoun they refer to).

> ANTECEDENT   PRON.
> *Many* of the people in Ubudu live *their* whole lives in poverty.

> ANTECEDENT   PRON.
> A *person* should love *his* parents.

>   ANTECEDENT   PRON.
> Great *music* can inspire and move people with *its* beauty.

2. The following indefinite pronouns are singular and take singular pronouns: *each*, *either*, *neither*, *one* and all words ending in -*one*, -*body*, or -*thing*, such as *anybody*, *nothing*, and *everybody*.

> ANTECEDENT   PRON.
> *Each* of the women took off *her* hat.

*Note to student: It is advisable to study this section *after* you study *Subject-Verb Agreement*, page 189.

ANTECEDENT   PRON.
Everyone should bring *his* book to class.

ANTECEDENT
I knew *one* of the students, but I could not remember

PRON.
her name.

ANTECEDENT   PRON.
Nobody in that office knows what *he* is supposed to do.

ANTECEDENT   PRON.
Everyone in the class should do *her* own work

PRON.
herself.

3. When compound subjects are joined by *neither . . . nor* or *either
    . . . or*, the pronoun will agree with the subject nearer the verb.

    S   S *(nearer the verb)*   PRON.
    Neither my *mother* nor my *sisters* could lend me *their*
    sewing machine.

    S   S *(nearer the verb)* PRON.
    Either my *sisters* or my *mother* will lend me *her*
    typewriter.

4. Some words appear to be plural but are actually singular. Some
    of these are: *physics*, *mathematics*, *economics*, *news*, and *politics*.

    ANTECEDENT   PRON.
    Politics interests me as *it* affects the economy.

ERROR EXAMPLES

A. WRONG: Modern music, including disco and rock n'roll, reflects
            modern society in their themes and musical qualities.
    RIGHT: Modern music, including disco and rock n' roll, reflects
            modern society in *its* themes and musical qualities.
            (The antecedent of *its* is *music*.)

B. WRONG: Every woman can find their place in the world.
    RIGHT: Every woman can find *her* place in the world.
            (The antecedent of *her* is *woman*.)

C. WRONG: Neither the stars nor the moon shone their light on us.
    RIGHT: Neither the stars nor the moon shone *its* light on us.
            (The antecedent of *its* is *moon*.)

D. WRONG: Either Paul or his parents will let me use his car.
    RIGHT: Either Paul or his parents will let me use *their* car.
             (The antecedent of *their* is *parents*.)

E. WRONG: Every one of the students wrote their names on the paper.
    RIGHT: Every one of the students wrote *his name* on the paper.
             (The antecedent of *his* is *one*.)

F. WRONG: Each of the boys should have their teeth checked.
    RIGHT: Each of the boys should have *his* teeth checked.
             (The antecedent of *his* is *each*.)

G. WRONG: Neither of the girls had remembered to bring their notebook.
    RIGHT: Neither of the girls had remembered to bring *her* notebook.
             (The antecedent of *her* is *neither*.)

H. WRONG: I asked everybody to do their best.
    RIGHT: I asked everybody to do *his or her* best.
             (The antecedent of *his or her* is *everybody*.)

I. WRONG: Did anybody do the work themselves?
    RIGHT: Did anybody do the work *himself?*
             (The antecedent of *himself* is *anybody*.)

J. WRONG: Mathematics has always interested me with their concrete yet abstract nature.
    RIGHT: Mathematics has always interested me with *its* concrete yet abstract nature.
             (The antecedent of *its* is *mathematics*.)

EXERCISE: Put "C" if the sentence is correct. Put "X" if there is an error in number agreement of a pronoun and its antecedent.

_____1. Every one of my girl friends has given their opinion of me.

_____2. Every person who asked was permitted to bring his or her book to class to use during the examination.

_____3. Neither the doctor nor her patients had an opportunity to express their feelings.

_____4. I am looking for a person who has forgotten their suitcase.

_____5. Each of the children may use the swimming pool if he promises to be careful.

_____6. Neither my sisters nor my mother has remembered her promise to me.

_____7. Many of the students explained his situation to me personally.

_____8. If anybody is in the office, they will answer their telephone.

_____9. If everybody who had come to the meeting had brought their report with them, the meeting would have gone a lot more smoothly.

_____10. Neither the cat nor the dogs will eat the food I bought for him.

_____11. One of my daughters has left her purse on the coffee table.

_____12. Neither of the police officers was willing to give me his name.

_____13. The news from that country is well known for their objectivity.

_____14. Either the boss or her workers will have to give a little of their time to solve this problem.

_____15. Great works of art, such as the *Mona Lisa* and *Whistler's Mother*, can be deceptive in their simplicity.

_____16. One sometimes gives up something they want for the sake of others.

_____17. One of the first students to come into the room could not find his name on the list.

_____18. Nobody lost their patience even though the meeting was long and boring.

_____19. Everybody must pay their fair share towards the gift.

_____20. All of my friends brought their husbands with them to my party.

Check your answers with the error key on page 130.

PRONOUNS—*THOSE* MODIFIED

The demonstrative pronoun *those* can be followed by a phrase or clause that modifies it.

No one is allowed in the room except *those*

CLAUSE
who have paid.

PHRASE
Those waiting to see the doctor may go in now.

NOTE:

The *personal* pronouns *they* and *them* should not be modified by a phrase or clause.

ERROR EXAMPLES

A. WRONG: They who need a receipt should sign here.
   RIGHT: *Those* who need a receipt should sign here.

B. WRONG: For them interested in learning, the university offers a good program.
   RIGHT: For *those* interested in learning, the university offers a good program.

C. WRONG: We invited only them we like to the party.
   RIGHT: We invited only *those* we like to the party.

EXERCISE: Put "C" if the sentence is correct. Put "X" if there is an error in the demonstrative pronouns.

_____1. She told her secret to only those she trusted.

_____2. He will consider hiring only them currently studying art.

_____3. The police turned the crowd away since only they with a permit could protest.

_____4. Please send this pamphlet to those who have expressed an interest in this study.

_____5. This line is for them with discount coupons.

_____6. For them of you who appreciate good music, there is an excellent concert this evening.

_____7. For them who like to travel to a warm place, Fiji is a paradise.

_____8. The chairman of the board will talk to those whom he has already interviewed.

_____9. Those who wish to bring their children to the party may do so.

_____10. They who arrive early will get the best selection of seats.

Check your answers with the error key on page 131.

CHAPTER QUIZ—Pronouns

DIRECTIONS: Put "C" if the sentence is correct.
Put "X" if there is an error with the pronoun.

_____1. When one has many problems, he should try to solve them one at a time.

_____2. Mary could never understand him wanting to be a nurse.

_____3. I often think back to the time when mutual friends introduced Paul and I.

_____4. Claire noticed many people who had been waiting hours to buy their tickets.

_____5. When the children realized that they were by theirselves in the dark, they became really frightened.

_____6. In the course of life one should always remember their old friends.

_____7. Do you remember the teacher that his daughter became a doctor?

_____8. For them of you who wish to know more about journalism, we recommend that you order a book from the following list.

_____9. Neither my aunt nor my cousins were able to explain their behavior.

_____10. Mary was surprised to realize that it was us, her old school friends, calling her from Paris.

_____11. The dean asked all the students, including Betty and I, to show our visitor every possible courtesy.

_____12. Give the refunds to those who have filled out the correct form.

_____13. They say that English can be a very difficult language for one to learn in his later years.

_____14. Modern society, including conservatives, liberals, hippies, and blacks, has many problems that they must solve.

_____15. Elaine met the actress who you admire so much.

_____16. Bob called to his old friend John as he walked across the campus.

TOEFL Grammar Workbook

_____17. In the paper it says it is going to rain today.

_____18. Did you ever see a man as tall as he?

_____19. Neither of the girls remembered to give I her notebook.

_____20. I am worried about your having to review so much material.

Check your answers with the error key on page 131.

ERROR KEYS

PRONOUNS—Relatives

ERROR KEY

__X__ 1. (novels *which* deal) OR (novels *that* deal). See rules 2 and 3.

__X__ 2. (a man *whose* experience). See rule 4.

__C__ 3.

__X__ 4. (a dress *which*) OR (a dress *that*). See rules 2 and 3.

__C__ 5.

__C__ 6.

__X__ 7. (a man *who*) OR (a man *that*). See rules 1 and 3.

__C__ 8.

__X__ 9. (the baby *who*) OR (the baby *that*). See rules 1 and 3.

__X__ 10. (woman *whose* photograph). See rule 4.

PRONOUNS—Personal—Case

ERROR KEY

__X__ 1. (Betty and *he* were hurt). See rule 1.

__C__ 2.

__X__ 3. (by *himself*). See note c.

__X__ 4. (Margaret and *me*). See rule 2 and note a.

__C__ 5.

__X__ 6. (of Susan and *her*). See rule 2.

__C__ 7.

__C__ 8.

__C__ 9.

_X_ 10. (my husband or *me*). See rule 2.

_X_ 11. (by *themselves*). See note c.

_X_ 12. (as intelligent as *he*). See note b.

_C_ 13.

_C_ 14.

_X_ 15. (It is *she*). See rule 1.

PRONOUNS—WHO/WHOM

ERROR KEY

_X_ 1. (*who* I thought were). See rules 1a and 2.

_X_ 2. (*whom* you trust). See rule 1b.

_C_ 3.

_X_ 4. (*whom* I think you met). See rules 1b and 2.

_C_ 5.

_X_ 6. (*whom* the teacher chose). See rule 1b.

_C_ 7.

_C_ 8.

_X_ 9. (*who* do you think will). See rules 1a and 2.

_C_ 10.

_X_ 11. (*who* handled). See rule 1a.

_X_ 12. (to *whomever* you like). See rule 1b.

_X_ 13. (*whoever* answers). See rule 1a.

_C_ 14.

_X_ 15. (*who* are working). See rule 1a.

PRONOUNS—Possessives

ERROR KEY

_C_ 1.

_X_ 2. (*your* saying good-bye)

C 3.
C 4.
X 5. (*their* leaving)
X 6. (*its* meowing). See note.
X 7. (*His* playing)
C 8.
C 9.
X 10. (*my* having to drive)
C 11.
X 12. (*his* winning)
C 13.
X 14. (*our* whispering)
X 15. (*my* taking)

PRONOUNS—Faulty Reference

ERROR KEY

X 1. (*Mr. Smith* told Mr. Jones, "*I* have lost). See error example A.

X 2. (*The telephone directory* says). See error example E.

C 3.

X 4. (As *Cathy* was driving home from work, *she* saw her friend.) See error example B.

X 5. (*the picture* looked strange). See error example D.

C 6.

X 7. (and *the stock market* suffered). See error example D.

C 8.

X 9. (*The newspaper* says). See error example E.

X 10. (and now *the A Team* is in first place). See error example C.

PRONOUNS—Person

ERROR KEY

_X_ 1. (*he* feels). See error example A and note A.

_C_ 2.

_X_ 3. (*one's* rent). See error example C.

_C_ 4.

_C_ 5.

_X_ 6. (*he* must). See error example A.

_X_ 7. (*one meets*) OR (*he meets*). See error example B and note a.

_C_ 8.

_C_ 9.

_X_ 10. (when *one finds oneself*). See error example B.

PRONOUNS—Number

ERROR KEY

_X_ 1. (*her* opinion). The antecedent of *her* is *one*. See rule 2.

_C_ 2.

_C_ 3.

_X_ 4. (*his* suitcase). The antecedent of *his* is *person*. See rule 1.

_C_ 5.

_C_ 6.

_X_ 7. (*their* situation). The antecedent of *their* is *many*. See rule 1.

_X_ 8. (*he* will answer *his* telephone) The antecedent of *he* and *his* is *anybody*. See rule 2.

_X_ 9. (*his* report with *him*). The antecedent of *his* and *him* is *everybody*. See rule 2.

_X_ 10. (for *them*). The antecedent of *them* is *dogs*. See rule 3.

_C_ 11.

_C_ 12.

_X_ 13. (for *its* objectivity). The antecedent of *its* is *news*. See rule 4.

_C_ 14.

_C_ 15.

_X_ 16. (*one* wants) OR (*he* wants). The antecedent of *one* or *he* is *one*. See rule 2.

_C_ 17.

_X_ 18. (*his* patience). The antecedent of *his* is *nobody*. See rule 2.

_X_ 19. (*his* fair share). The antecedent of *his* is *everybody*. See rule 2.

_C_ 20.

PRONOUNS—THOSE Modified

ERROR KEY

_C_ 1.

_X_ 2. (*those* currently studying art)

_X_ 3. (*those* with a permit)

_C_ 4.

_X_ 5. (*those* with discount coupons)

_X_ 6. (*those* of you who appreciate good music)

_X_ 7. (*those* who like to travel)

_C_ 8.

_C_ 9.

_X_ 10. (*Those* who arrive early)

CHAPTER QUIZ—Pronouns

ERROR KEY

_C_ 1.

_X_ 2. (*his* wanting). See *Possessives*, page 114.

_X_ 3. (Paul and *me*). See *Personal—Case*, page 109.

_C_ 4.

_X_5. (by *themselves*). See *Personal—Case*, page 109.

_X_6. (*one's* old friends) OR (*his* old friends). See *Person*, page 117.

_X_7. (teacher *whose* daughter). See *Relatives*, page 107.

_X_8. (For *those* of you). See <u>*Those Modified*</u>, page 122.

_C_9.

_X_10. (it was *we*). See *Personal—Case*, page 109.

_X_11. (including Betty and *me*). See *Personal—Case*, page 109.

_C_12.

_C_13.

_X_14. (*it* must solve). See *Number*, page 119.

_X_15. (*whom* you admire). See <u>*Who*/*Whom*</u>, page 111.

_X_16. (As Bob walked across the campus, he called to his old friend John.). See *Faulty Reference*, page 116.

_X_17. (*The paper says*). See *Faulty Reference*, page 116.

_C_18.

_X_19. (to give *me*). See *Personal—Case*, page 109.

_C_20.

XI

BASIC PATTERNS

BASIC PATTERNS—INDIRECT OBJECTS

Some verbs may be followed by two objects (an indirect object and a direct object). The following shows the patterns used when verbs take two objects.

1. Some verbs may use the following two patterns:

I.O.   D.O.

My father often gives *me* a *gift*.

OR

D.O. + TO + OBJ.

My father often gives a *gift to me*.

Some other verbs like *give* are: *bring*, *send*, *offer*, *pass*, *take*, *tell*, *read*, *write*, *teach*, *sell*.

2. Some verbs may use the following two patterns:

I.O.   D.O.

John usually buys *Mary* a *gift*.

OR

D.O. + FOR + OBJ.

John usually buys a *gift for Mary*.

Some other verbs like *buy* are: *fix*, *make*, *get*.

3. Some verbs use only the following pattern:

D.O. + TO + OBJ.
He explained his idea to us.

Some other verbs like explain are: announce, describe, deliver, mention, say, report, return.

4. Some verbs may use only the following pattern:

I.O.   D.O.
I asked Mary a question.

Some other verbs like ask are: cost, charge.

ERROR EXAMPLES

A. **WRONG:** Susan's friend sent to her a beautiful silk dress from China.

    RIGHT: Susan's friend sent her a beautiful silk dress from China.

OR

    Susan's friend sent a beautiful silk dress to her from China.

B. **WRONG:** John fixed the broken lamp to Harold.

    RIGHT: John fixed the broken lamp for Harold.

C. **WRONG:** The professor explained me the difficult point of grammar.

    RIGHT: The professor explained the difficult point of grammar to me.

D. **WRONG:** The new suit cost over forty dollars to me.

    RIGHT: The new suit cost me over forty dollars.

E. **WRONG:** The store charged over fifteen dollars to me to alter the jacket I bought.

    RIGHT: The store charged me over fifteen dollars to alter the jacket I bought.

EXERCISE: Put "C" if the sentence is correct. Put "X" if there is an indirect object error.

_____1. We returned the defective merchandise to the store immediately.

_____2. I hope you will write to me long letters while you are away.

_____3. When do you think you can deliver them the package?

_____4. That is the third time you have asked me the same question.

_____5. My mother is making for Mary a new skirt.

_____6. Please pass the potatoes to me after you take some.

_____7. The belt buckle cost over ten dollars to Bob.

_____8. He taught to me everything he knew.

_____9. When she was abroad, Laura got several pairs of earrings for her mother.

_____10. He sent me a beautiful letter from Spain.

Check your answers with the answer key on page 151.

BASIC PATTERNS—ORDER OF ADVERBS

1. In general, place adverbs (or adverbial phrases) after the verb or after the object, if any. (Do not separate the subject from the verb or the verb from its object.)

The two patterns are:

a) Subject + verb + adverb

    S + VERB + ADV.
    He works here.

b) Subject + verb + object + adverb or adverbial phrase

    He wants to eat soon.

    S + VERB + OBJ.   ADV. PHRASE
    We see them from time to time.

2. Some adverbs can come before a single-word verb or the main verb.

        ADV.   VERB
    He promptly left the room.

ADV.   MAIN VERB
He was *quickly escorted* from the room.

3. Single-word adverbs of frequency usually come after the verb *to be* and before a single-word verb or the main verb. (Note: Common adverbs of frequency are: *often, rarely, sometimes, frequently, occasionally, ever, never, seldom, usually, always*.)

BE   ADV.
He *is never* on time.

ADV. VERB
I *often see* her.

ADV.   MAIN VERB
I had *frequently noticed* her.

4. *Still* comes before a single-word verb or the main verb in affirmative sentences and before the auxiliary in negative sentences.

MAIN VERB
He is *still waiting* for you.

AUX.
He *still has* not answered my questions.

5. In general, the order of final adverbs is *place* and then *time*.

PLACE   TIME
He went *to Europe last summer.*

PLACE   TIME
I saw him *at the library last night*.

ERROR EXAMPLES

A. WRONG: John in the classroom is waiting.
    RIGHT: John is waiting *in the classroom.*

B. WRONG: Betty is writing in her bedroom letters.
    RIGHT: Betty is writing letters *in her bedroom.*

C. WRONG: Alex played with great passion the piano.
    RIGHT: Alex played the piano *with great passion.*

D. WRONG: I write sometimes letters to my parents.
    RIGHT: I *sometimes* write letters to my parents.

E.   WRONG: John waited seldom for me.
     RIGHT: John *seldom* waited for me.

F.   WRONG: He rarely is on time.
     RIGHT: He is *rarely* on time.

G.   WRONG: Bob prepares once in a while dinner.
     RIGHT: Bob prepares dinner *once in a while*.

H.   WRONG: She bought yesterday several new dresses.
     RIGHT: She bought several new dresses *yesterday*.

I.   WRONG: They wrote during the summer to us.
     RIGHT: They wrote to us *during the summer*.

J.   WRONG: He sold immediately the gold watch.
     RIGHT: He sold the gold watch *immediately*.

K.   WRONG: He has read before that book.
     RIGHT: He has read that book *before*.

L.   WRONG: He is studying still in the library.
     RIGHT: He is *still* studying in the library.

M.   WRONG: They have not still finished.
     RIGHT: They *still* have not finished.

N.   WRONG: He sent his daughter in the summer to college.
     RIGHT: He sent his daughter *to college in the summer*.

EXERCISE: Put "C" if the sentence is correct. Put "X" if there is an error in the placement of the adverb.

_____1.   He hopes to Rome to be able to go.

_____2.   The doctor sees patients only in the afternoon.

_____3.   David last evening went to the movies.

_____4.   He executed with verve the difficult piano passage.

_____5.   He found several useful books in my bookcase.

_____6.   He wants still to move to London next year.

_____7.   I observe frequently his behavior.

_____8.   He recently met with his new advisor.

_____9.   Tom lately has been working on his new book.

_____10.   He was suddenly amused by her spontaneity.

_____11.   He wrote usually in that unconventional style.

_____12.   They still do not appreciate their good luck.

_____13. Jill during her college years lived in France.

_____14. Has he seen the city before?

_____15. Karl still has not remembered where he put his keys.

_____16. The teacher posted on her office door her office hours.

_____17. He is often accused of not being a serious person.

_____18. Betty noticed rarely my hard work.

_____19. John last night telephoned me.

_____20. He went to the kitchen in the middle of the night for a glass of water.

Check your answers with the error key on page 151.

BASIC PATTERNS— EMBEDDED QUESTIONS

1. The pattern for an embedded question in a statement is *question word + subject + verb* or *question word/subject* (same word) *+ verb*.

   QW + S + V
   I cannot see *what the sign says*.

   QW + S + V
   She does not know *where she should go*.

   QW/S + V
   They did not know *who bought the car*.

2. The pattern for an embedded question in a question is the same as for an embedded question in a statement. (See rule 1.)

   QW + S + V
   Do you know *who he is*?

   QW/S + V
   Did he say *who called*?

3. Do not use *do*, *does*, or *did* as auxiliaries in these patterns.

ERROR EXAMPLES

A. WRONG: I did not understand what did they mean.
   RIGHT: I did not understand what *they meant*.

B. WRONG: Do you know where is John?
   RIGHT: Do you know where *John is*?

C. WRONG: I was surprised when he told me how much does he study every day.
   RIGHT: I was surprised when he told me how much *he studies* every day.

D. WRONG: He told me when was he free during the week.
   RIGHT: He told me when *he was* free during the week.

E. WRONG: Tell me where they do go after class every day.
   RIGHT: Tell me where *they go* after class every day.

EXERCISE: Put "C" if the sentence is correct. Put "X" if there is an error in the pattern for embedded questions.

_____1. I will ask how much do they sell for.

_____2. Did the professor tell you when is the next test?

_____3. I wonder when it is going to begin.

_____4. Forget about where we are going to play tennis as it is starting to rain.

_____5. Did you see what did he do?

_____6. Do you remember how much the tuition was?

_____7. Ask the operator what is the charge for a three-minute call to New York.

_____8. We don't know when will we see our friends again.

_____9. He forgot where he parked his car.

_____10. Would you please ask them where is the subway entrance.

_____11. He sent a telegram saying when he would arrive.

_____12. I forgot to ask him what time does the class begin.

_____13. Bill did not realize what time it was when I knocked on the door.

_____14. Can you tell us who that distinguished-looking gentleman is?

_____15. Ask Mr. Blake what does his daughter study at the university.

_____16. Can you be sure where will he be this Friday afternoon?

_____17. We should find out how hot is it in the summer before we decide to vacation there.

_____18. Can anyone explain why he had that terrible attitude?

_____19. We never found the village where were born our parents.

_____20. She does not know who did paint that beautiful mural.

Check your answers with the error key on page 152.

BASIC PATTERNS—*TO/FOR* (PURPOSE)

Patterns for expressing purpose:

1. *for* + noun phrase

N PHRASE
John went to California *for* a *rest*.

2. *to* + simple form of the verb (that is, the infinitive)

TO + VERB
John went to California *to ski*.

ERROR EXAMPLES

A. **WRONG:** She moved to New York for getting a better job.
   RIGHT: She moved to New York *to get* a better job.

OR

   RIGHT: She moved to New York *for* a better job.

B. **WRONG:** They went to the country for having a vacation.
   RIGHT: They went to the country *for a* vacation.

OR

   RIGHT: They went to the country *to have* a vacation.

C. WRONG: We used the projector for to show a movie.
   RIGHT: We used the projector *to show* a movie.

EXERCISE: Put "C" if the sentence is correct. Put "X" if there is a *to/for* (purpose) error.

_____1. He went to the lecture for hearing about the latest agricultural techniques.

_____2. They studied hard to pass the TOEFL.

_____3. We saved money this year for to take a trip to Hong Kong.

_____4. They bought that book for trying to learn Japanese.

_____5. He is studying for a master's degree in marketing.

_____6. I came to the United States for to visit my relatives.

_____7. She is desperately looking for work.

_____8. John went to the doctor's office for his yearly check-up.

_____9. Let's go shopping this afternoon for finding some camping equipment for our trip.

_____10. Susan went to the printer's office to order some wedding invitations.

Check your answers with the error key on page 153.

BASIC PATTERNS—DOUBLE SUBJECTS

Do not use a noun *and* a pronoun as a subject. Only one is necessary.

    s
He saw my uncle the other day.

      s
The *woman* in the red dress is my teacher.

    s
It is easy to see from here.

ERROR EXAMPLES

A. WRONG: My brother he is always borrowing my car.
    RIGHT: My *brother is* always borrowing my car.

B. WRONG: Their method of teaching it is very good.
    RIGHT: Their method of *teaching is* very good.

C. WRONG: I could not believe that my boyfriend he told me a lie.
    RIGHT: I could not believe that my *boyfriend told* me a lie.

EXERCISE: Put "C" if the sentence is correct. Put "X" if there is a double-subject error.

_____1. That subject it has always been difficult for me.

_____2. I could not believe it when my boss gave me a raise.

_____3. That is the man who he told me the bad news.

_____4. They told me that their uncle was arriving this afternoon.

_____5. You and I we always have a good time together.

_____6. The TOEFL test it is a real challenge.

_____7. That lobster is delicious because it is so fresh.

_____8. Carol said that she and her sister they had bought a new car.

_____9. The president was acquitted in the scandal.

_____10. Your husband had a good excuse for arriving late.

Check your answers with the error key on page 153.

BASIC PATTERNS—CLAUSES

INDEPENDENT CLAUSES

1. Every sentence must have at least one independent clause. An independent clause consists of at least one subject and one finite verb (see note c) and is a complete thought. The following are examples of independent clauses:

     S   V
The *president spoke*.

   S   V
Betty made some iced tea.

  S V
He is a doctor.

  S   V
They arrived at 2:00.

 S V
I was there.

2. Two independent clauses can be joined by *and*, *but*, *or*, *nor*, or *for*.

    S   V   S   V
He went to the bank, <u>*but*</u> *it was* closed.

    S   V   S   V
She had never *been* to Los Angeles before, <u>*and*</u> *she was*
quite surprised at the rush-hour traffic jams.

DEPENDENT CLAUSES

3. A sentence may have one or more dependent clauses, each one
of which must have its own subject and finite verb. A dependent
clause must be attached to an independent clause. It is incomplete
by itself. There are three kinds of dependent clauses: noun,
relative (adjective), and adverb.

    a) A noun clause functions as a subject or an object. Each
       noun clause, which has its own subject and verb, may be
       an embedded statement or an embedded question.

         1) Embedded statements are often introduced by
            that.

                S   V
            That <u>*he was*</u> a *criminal* surprised me.
            (*N cl. as S*)

                            S V
            I know (*that*) <u>*he is*</u> from Canada.   (*N cl.*
            as obj.)

         2) Embedded questions are introduced by *wh*-words.

I do not know *what time the party begins*.
(N cl. as obj.)

He talked about *what he had learned in his class*. (N cl. as obj. of prep.)

b) A relative clause functions as an adjective. Each relative clause, which has its own subject and verb, is introduced by one of the following words: *who, whom, which, that,* and *whose.*

I do not know the lady *who lives next door.*

He is a man *(whom)* I respect.*

That is a fern plant, *which never blooms.*

This is the book *(that)* I borrowed from John.*

That is the couple *whose house burned down.*

*Note: *Whom* and *that*, when used as objects, are optional.

c) An adverb clause functions as an adverb. Each adverb clause has its own subject and verb. The following is a list of commonly used words that introduce adverb clauses: *before, after, because, since, while, when, if,* and *although.* Introductory adverb clauses are followed by a comma.

Before she left, I told her.

When it began to rain, we left.

If I have time, I will help you.

Although he tried hard, he did not win the race.

We talked to her *after she had surgery.*

He did not go in *because he was late.*

$$\overset{S}{}\overset{V}{}$$

I have not seen him *since he arrived*.

$$\overset{S}{}\overset{V}{}$$

They met him *when they were* at college.

NOTES:

a. Be sure that every dependent clause is attached to an independent clause.

b. Remember that all clauses, independent and dependent, have their own subject and finite verb.

c. A finite verb is one that can be conjugated and shows tense, that is, ends in *-ed*, *-s*, etc. A gerund (V + *ing*) or an infinitive (*to* + V) is not a finite verb.

d. In this grammar explanation, when any word appears in parenthesis, it is optional in the sentence.

e. Remember that two independent clauses are joined by coordinate conjunctions (*and*, *but*, etc.). They cannot be joined by a comma only.

===

ERROR EXAMPLES

A. WRONG: Give my regards to everyone asks about me.
    RIGHT: Give my regards to everyone *who* asks about me.

B. WRONG: Thinking for many centuries that the world was flat.
    RIGHT: *It was thought* for many centuries that the world was flat.

C. WRONG: President Kennedy committed the U.S. to being first to land men on the moon, he died before he saw his dream realized.
    RIGHT: President Kennedy committed the U.S. to being first to land men on the moon, *but* he died before he saw his dream realized.

D. WRONG: To believe that smoking causes some forms of cancer.
    RIGHT: *It is believed* that smoking causes some forms of cancer.

E. WRONG: That Mt. Everest is the highest peak in the world.
    RIGHT: *I know that* Mt. Everest is the highest peak in the world.
                        OR
            Mt. Everest is the highest peak in the world.

F. **WRONG:** Because I did not have enough money to go on vacation this year.

   RIGHT: Because I did not have enough money to go on vacation this year, *I stayed home*.

   OR

   I did not have enough money to go on vacation this year.

G. **WRONG:** We were surprised when saw her.

   RIGHT: We were surprised when *we saw* her.

H. **WRONG:** Where they would be staying in Greece.

   RIGHT: *She told me* where they would be staying in Greece.

EXERCISE: Put "C" if the sentence is correct. Put "X" if there is a clause error.

_____1. It is hoped that man will someday inhabit other planets.

_____2. Learning that the university plans to construct a new sports arena next year.

_____3. Since it was cool and overcast, we canceled the picnic.

_____4. Why he quit his job with that prestigious company.

_____5. Some people consider marriage to be the most important thing could happen in life.

_____6. That Columbus was not the first man to set foot in the New World.

_____7. He found the book he had been looking for under the sofa.

_____8. We went to San Diego, we spent many happy hours on the beach.

_____9. To think that everyone needs some form of physical exercise.

_____10. The store had a huge end-of-summer sale, and hundreds of people were at the door when it opened.

_____11. If any questions, please ask me for help.

_____12. That he survived that terrible accident surprised everyone who heard the news.

_____13. There is the artist whose painting received an award.

_____14. She is the only person in this country knows how to operate that new equipment.

_____15. I noticed that the new couple next door not at home last week.

Check your answers with the error key on page 154.

CHAPTER QUIZ—Basic Patterns

DIRECTIONS: Choose the best answer (A, B, C, or D) to complete each of the following sentences. Put the letter of the best choice in the space provided.

_____1. _____ is indispensable to the economy of that region.

    (A) That copper mining
    (B) It is copper mining
    (C) Although copper mining
    (D) Copper mining

_____2. She read _____.

    (A) several chapters in the library last night
    (B) last night several chapters in the library
    (C) last night in the library several chapters
    (D) in the library several chapters last night

_____3. Doris went to the nicest store in the city _____ presents for her children.

    (A) for to get
    (B) for getting
    (C) to get
    (D) to getting

_____4. The man on the horse_____ a famous movie star.

    (A) he is
    (B) is he
    (C) who is
    (D) is

_____5. Please do not ever mention _____.

    (A) that subject again to us
    (B) that subject to us again
    (C) to us that subject again
    (D) again to us that subject

_____6. She cannot remember where _____ her black
jacket.

(A) did she leave
(B) she did leave
(C) she left
(D) left she

_____7. The doctor explained _____ that we should have
a complete physical examination once a year.

(A) us
(B) for us
(C) to us
(D) at us

_____8. Would you please tell us _____.

(A) when the next bus comes
(B) when comes the next bus
(C) when does the next bus come
(D) when the next bus does come

_____9. That attractive man _____ my cousin who is
visiting us from France.

(A) who is
(B) he is
(C) is
(D) is he

_____10. They _____ to our proposal.

(A) have not still responded
(B) have not responded still
(C) have still not responded
(D) still have not responded

_____

DIRECTIONS: Put the letter of the *incorrect*
answer in the space provided.

_____1. I did not understand their predicament until John explained
                              A   B

me   all the details of the mishap.
C   D

_____2. Even though we <u>had been</u> to her house several times be-
                         A

fore, we <u>did not remember</u> exactly <u>what</u> street <u>was it</u> on.
              B   C   D

_____3. We <u>are never</u> happy with <u>what</u> we have in life; the grass
              A   B

<u>always</u> is <u>greener</u> on the other side of the fence.
  C   D

_____4. The opera, <u>even though</u> performed <u>by</u> amateurs, <u>it</u> <u>was</u>
                  A   B   C D

excellent.

_____5. Because of their <u>countries'</u> great need for expertise <u>in</u> com-
                   A   B

puter programming, the students <u>were sent</u> <u>for studying</u> in
                                  C   D

the United States.

_____6. Mr. Shimoto was planning <u>to send</u> <u>to me</u> a package from
                                A   B

Japan <u>as soon as</u> he arrived <u>home</u> from his trip to Hawaii.
        C   D

_____7. I was surprised <u>to hear</u> that the store charged <u>Dr. Brown</u>
                 A   B

an extra amount <u>when it delivered</u> <u>to his office</u> his
                  C   D

new sofa.

_____8. When John asked Tomoko, the Japanese student, what she
<u>did think</u> of the museum, she <u>quickly</u> replied that it
  A   B

<u>had taught</u> her a great deal <u>about</u> the history of the area.
  C   D

_____ 9. His father mentioned <u>to me</u> that Robert <u>had written</u> <u>to him</u>
                                A   B   C

requesting money <u>for buying</u> a new car.
                 D

_____ 10. The author of this new book <u>she</u> is planning <u>to write</u> a
                                       A   B

sequel <u>in order to capitalize</u> on the publicity <u>she</u> has
        C   D

received recently.

Check your answers with the error key on page 155.

═══════════════════════════════════════

ERROR KEYS

BASIC PATTERNS—Indirect Objects

ERROR KEY

__C__ 1.

__X__ 2. (*write me* long letters) OR (write long letters *to me*). See rule 1.

__X__ 3. (deliver the package *to them*). See rule 3.

__C__ 4.

__X__ 5. (is *making Mary* a new skirt) OR (is making a new skirt *for Mary*). See rule 2.

__C__ 6.

__X__ 7. (*cost Bob* over ten dollars). See rule 4.

__X__ 8. (*taught me* everything) OR (taught everything he knew *to me*). See rule 1.

__C__ 9.

__C__ 10.

BASIC PATTERNS—Order of Adverbs

ERROR KEY

__X__ 1. (He hopes to be able to go *to Rome*.). See rule 1, pattern 2.

__C__ 2.

__X__ 3. (David went to the movies *last evening*.). See rule 1, pattern a and rule 5.

__X__ 4. (He executed the difficult piano passage *with verve*.). See rule 1, pattern b.

__C__ 5.

__X__ 6. (He *still* wants). See rule 4.

___X___ 7.   (I *frequently* observe). See rule 3.

___C___ 8.

___X___ 9.   (Tom has been working on his new book *lately*.). See rule 1, pattern b.

___C___ 10.

___X___ 11. (He *usually* wrote). See rule 3.

___C___ 12.

___X___ 13. (Jill lived in France *during her college years*.). See rule 1, pattern a and rule 5.

___C___ 14.

___C___ 15.

___X___ 16. (The teacher posted her office hours *on her office door*.). See rule 1, pattern b.

___C___ 17.

___X___ 18. (Betty *rarely* noticed my hard work.). See rule 3.

___X___ 19. (John telephoned me *last night*.). See rule 1, pattern b.

___C___ 20.

BASIC PATTERNS—Embedded Questions

ERROR KEY

___X___ 1.   (*how much they sell for*). See rule 3.

___X___ 2.   (*when the next test is?*). See rule 2.

___C___ 3.

___C___ 4.

___X___ 5.   (*what he did?*). See rule 3.

___C___ 6.

___X___ 7.   (*what the charge is*). See rule 1.

___X___ 8.   (*when we will see*). See rule 1.

___C___ 9.

___X___ 10. (*where the subway entrance is*). See rule 1.

___C___ 11.

X 12. (*what time the class begins*). See rule 3.

C 13.

C 14.

X 15. (*what his daughter studies*). See rule 3.

X 16. (*where he will be*). See rule 2.

X 17. (*how hot it is*). See rule 1.

C 18.

X 19. (*where our parents were born*). See rule 1.

X 20. (*who painted*). See rule 3.

BASIC PATTERNS—TO/FOR   (Purpose)

ERROR KEY

X 1. (*to hear*). See rule 2.

C 2.

X 3. (year *to take* a trip) OR (year *for a trip*). See rules 1 and 2.

X 4. (book *to try* to learn). See rule 2.

C 5.

X 6. (United States *to visit*). See rule 2.

C 7.

C 8.

X 9. (*to find*). See rule 2.

C 10.

BASIC PATTERNS—Double Subjects

ERROR KEY

X 1. (*subject has* always)

C 2.

X 3. (*who told* me)

_C_ 4.

_X_ 5. (*You and I always*) OR (*We always*)

_X_ 6. (*test is* a real)

_C_ 7.

_X_ 8. (she and her *sister had bought*)

_C_ 9.

_C_ 10.

BASIC PATTERNS—Clauses

ERROR KEY

_C_ 1.

_X_ 2. (*It was learned* that). See rule 3a (1) and note b.

_C_ 3.

_X_ 4. (*I cannot understand why* he quit his job.). See rule 3a (2) and note a.

_X_ 5. (thing *that* could). See rule 3b and note b.

_X_ 6. (*Columbus was not the first man to set foot in the New World.* OR *That Columbus was not the first man to set foot in the New World is not surprising.*) See rule 3a and note a.

_C_ 7.

_X_ 8. (Diego, *and* we spent). See rule 2 and note d.

_X_ 9. (*It is thought that*). See rule 3a (1) and notes b and c.

_C_ 10.

_X_ 11. (If *you have* any). See rule 3c and note b.

_C_ 12.

_C_ 13.

_X_ 14. (country *who* knows). See rule 3b and note b.

_X_ 15. (door *was* not). See rule 3a (1) and note b.

CHAPTER QUIZ—Basic Patterns

ERROR KEY

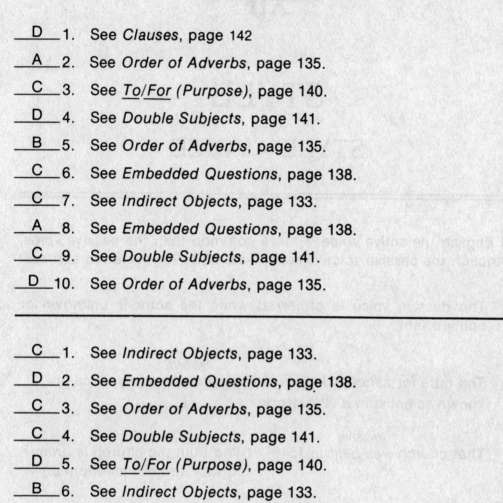

D 1. See *Clauses*, page 142

A 2. See *Order of Adverbs*, page 135.

C 3. See *To/For (Purpose)*, page 140.

D 4. See *Double Subjects*, page 141.

B 5. See *Order of Adverbs*, page 135.

C 6. See *Embedded Questions*, page 138.

C 7. See *Indirect Objects*, page 133.

A 8. See *Embedded Questions*, page 138.

C 9. See *Double Subjects*, page 141.

D 10. See *Order of Adverbs*, page 135.

C 1. See *Indirect Objects*, page 133.

D 2. See *Embedded Questions*, page 138.

C 3. See *Order of Adverbs*, page 135.

C 4. See *Double Subjects*, page 141.

D 5. See *To/For (Purpose)*, page 140.

B 6. See *Indirect Objects*, page 133.

D 7. See *Order of Adverbs*, page 135.

A 8. See *Embedded Questions*, page 138.

D 9. See *To/For (Purpose)*, page 140.

A 10. See *Double Subjects*, page 141.

XII

STYLE

STYLE—VOICE

In English the active voice is more common than the passive voice, although the passive voice is acceptable and even preferred at times.

1. The passive voice is preferred when the actor is unknown or unimportant.

    PASSIVE
    The cure for cancer *will* probably *be discovered* by some unknown scientist in a laboratory.

    PASSIVE
    That church *was built* in 1549.   (*Who* built the church is unimportant and not mentioned.)

2. The passive voice is often used when discussing history.

    PASSIVE
    The war *was fought* over gold.

3. Use the active voice when the actor is more important than the action.

    ACTORS ACTIVE
    The *children ate* spaghetti for dinner.

    ACTORS ACTIVE
    We watched the news.

4. Avoid using active and passive in the same sentence if possible.

PASSIVE   PASSIVE

The flowers *were planted* and the trees *were trimmed* .

ACTIVE   ACTIVE

Susan *cooked* the dinner and *washed* the dishes.

5. Use one verb instead of two when possible.

Rita enjoys good food and music.   (*Not*: Rita enjoys good food and music is also enjoyed by her.)

ERROR EXAMPLES

In the following examples we cannot say that the first sentence is absolutely *wrong*. In certain contexts it may even be preferred. However, generally speaking, the corrected sentence (the second sentence) is preferable. We are calling the first sentence AWKWARD and the second sentence BETTER.

A. AWKWARD: Ice cream was eaten at the party by the children.
   BETTER: The children ate ice cream at the party.

B. AWKWARD: Workers built the pyramids about 5,000 years ago.
   BETTER: The pyramids were built about 5,000 years ago.

C. AWKWARD: Some people painted pictures of animals on ancient cave walls.
   BETTER: Pictures of animals were painted on ancient cave walls.

D. AWKWARD: The house was bought by my mother and father in 1970.
   BETTER: My mother and father bought the house in 1970.

E. AWKWARD: Henry likes swimming and golfing is also liked by him.
   BETTER: Henry likes swimming and golfing.

F. AWKWARD: Sally loves children and her summers are spent working in a summer camp.
   BETTER: Sally loves children and spends her summers working in a summer camp.

G. AWKWARD: The rainbow was seen by us as the storm began to subside.
   BETTER: We saw the rainbow as the storm began to subside.

EXERCISE: Put "C" if the sentence seems correct as written. Put "A" (for awkward) if the choice of voice seems incorrect.

_____1. Steak was eaten by me last night.

_____2. When we work hard, we accomplish a lot.

_____3. Jane wrote a very good composition for her writing class.

_____4. We laughed when the clown fell out of the car.

_____5. Workers built the road in two years at a cost of five million dollars.

_____6. The people loved their leader and his mistakes were forgiven by them.

_____7. The phone was answered by John on the first ring.

_____8. Paul teaches English in high school and writes short stories in his free time.

_____9. Most American cars are built in Detroit, Michigan.

_____10. My uncle worked hard all his life and left a sizable estate when he died.

_____11. My father and I played chess for several hours yesterday.

_____12. As we neared the house, a small dog sitting on the porch could be seen by us.

_____13. Some people committed a lot of crimes in this neighborhood last month.

_____14. If you studied more, your tests could be easily passed.

_____15. The students opened their books and began to read.

_____16. As John approaches his fortieth birthday, he is reassessing the direction of his life.

_____17. The light was turned on by me as I entered my bedroom.

_____18. That electronics company is expanding and many new products are being developed by them.

_____19. Soldiers fought the Battle of Hastings in 1066.

_____20. Her earrings were put on by Jane before she went to the party.

_____21. During the war thousands of persons were forced to leave their homes.

_____22. Claire painted the living room and a new carpet was laid by her.

_____23. Jack works hard during the week and his free time is spent sailing his new boat.

_____24. The students were carefully selected and they represented the class well.

_____25. Bob plays the piano and the guitar is played by him also.

Check your answers with the error key on page 208.

STYLE—PARALLELISM

1. Items in a series must be parallel; that is, they must have the same grammatical form.

a) NOUNS

He likes *music*, *art*, and *history*.

b) GERUNDS

He likes *swimming*, *dancing*, and horseback *riding*.

c) ADJECTIVES

He is *tall*, *dark*, and *handsome*.

d) INFINITIVES

They wanted *to paint* the living room, *to lay* a new carpet, and *to buy* a new sofa.

Note: The preposition *to* may be omitted in the second and third infinitives.

e) PAST TENSE

The Romans *conquered*, *colonized*, and *governed* much of the world.

f)   **PAST PERFECT TENSE**

PAST PERF.   PAST PERF.
He *had finished* the game, *had taken* a shower, and

PAST PERF.
had eaten lunch by the time I got to his house.

Note: The auxiliary *had* may be omitted in the second and third verb phrases.

2.   Structures joined by *and*, *but*, *as*, *or*, *than*, or *although* must have the same grammatical form.

a)   **AND**

N PHRASE
He enjoyed *the music of Spain and*

N PHRASE
the sculpture of France.

b)   **BUT**

ADJ.   ADJ.
That verb form is not *active* , *but passive*.

c)   **AS**

V + ING   V + ING
Taking the bus can be as costly *as taking* a plane.

d)   **OR**

INFIN.   INFIN.
He wanted *to borrow* a car *or to rent* one while his car was being repaired.

e)   **THAN**

V + ING   V + ING
Eating in a restaurant is more fun *than cooking* at home.

f)   **ALTHOUGH**

INFIN.
Although he liked *to eat* good food, he did not like

INFIN.
to pay high prices for it.

ERROR EXAMPLES

A. WRONG: When they were in Mexico, they saw museums, ruins, and folk dancing.

  RIGHT: When they were in Mexico, they saw museums, ruins, and folk *dances*.

B. WRONG: He is young, intelligent, and has charm.

  RIGHT: He is young, intelligent, and *charming*.

C. WRONG: She likes to read, to travel, and painting.

  RIGHT: She likes to read, to travel, and *to paint*.

D. WRONG: They came out of the building hurriedly, hailed a cab, and jump into it.

  RIGHT: They came out of the building hurriedly, hailed a cab, and *jumped* into it.

E. WRONG: Her husband had bought a house, found a job, and chose a school for the children before she arrived.

  RIGHT: Her husband had bought a house, found a job, and *chosen* a school for the children before she arrived.

F. WRONG: We enjoyed the varied cuisine and going to the excellent theater in New York.

  RIGHT: We enjoyed the varied cuisine and *the excellent theater* in New York.

G. WRONG: That soup should not be served hot, but at a cold temperature.

  RIGHT: That soup should not be served hot, but *cold*.

H. WRONG: Renting an apartment can be as expensive as to buy a house.

  RIGHT: Renting an apartment can be as expensive as *buying* a house.

I. WRONG: He did not like to swim or skiing.

  RIGHT: He did not like to swim or *to ski*.

J. WRONG: Going on vacation is more fun than to work in the summer.

  RIGHT: Going on vacation is more fun than *working* in the summer.

EXERCISE: Put "C" if the sentence is correct. Put "X" if there is an error in parallelism.

_____1. When he was a college student, he learned to play tennis, to golf, and swimming.

_____2. Do not speak out, but raise your hand.

_____3. To face adversity, to solve problems, and to overcome difficulties all give one a sense of satisfaction.

_____4. We enjoyed the perfect weather and seeing fjords in Norway.

_____5. Go to Window A, ask for a form, and bring it back to me.

_____6. Before he died, he had sold his house, wrote a will, and set up a trust fund.

_____7. Her hobbies are reading, playing the piano, and gardening.

_____8. Being a homemaker is as difficult as working in an office.

_____9. After years of dealing with the public, she developed great charm, wit, and confident.

_____10. On their vacation they enjoyed swimming at the beach, walking through the quaint streets, and sitting in the picturesque parks.

_____11. He could not decide whether to get a job or studying.

_____12. Although he was quick to criticize, he was slow praising his students.

_____13. The presidential candidate was a man of intellectual strength, moral character, and personal integrity.

_____14. The bellhop took my bags to my room, opened the door, and puts them at the foot of the bed.

_____15. Jogging is more vigorous exercise than to play golf.

Check your answers with the error key on page 209.

STYLE—WORDINESS

A general rule in English might be that "shorter is better." That is, when the same idea can be expressed directly in fewer words, choose the shorter version. There are several ways to do this:

1. Avoid unnecessary passive constructions. See *Style—Voice*, page 156.

2. Avoid unnecessary relative clauses where an adjective, participial phrase, prepositional phrase, or appositive is enough.

ADJ.

The *tall* man bought the car.   (Not: The man *who is tall* bought the car.)

PART. PHRASE

The young girl *waiting by the door* would like to see you.   (Not: The young girl *who is waiting by the door* would like to see you.)

PREP. PHRASE

The package *on the table* is ready to be mailed.   (Not: The package *that is on the table* is ready to be mailed.)

APPOSITIVE

Hawaii, *the fiftieth state*, is a favorite vacation spot.   (Not: Hawaii, *which is the fiftieth* state, is a favorite vacation spot.)

3. Be as direct as possible.

It was an important discovery.   (Not: It was a discovery *of great importance*.)

He believed in God.   (Not: He believed in *the existence of a Supreme Being*.)

She did enzyme research from 1950 to 1964.   (Not: She spent a *total of fourteen years* from 1950 to 1964 *in the research area of enzymes*.)

He walked down the stairs quickly.   (Not: He walked down the stairs *in a quick manner*.)

4.   Avoid redundancy (repetition of the same idea).

She returned on Monday.   (Not: He returned *back* on Monday.)

His virtue was well known.   (Not: His virtue *and goodness* were well known. *Virtue* is *goodness*.)

ERROR EXAMPLES

In the following examples we cannot say that the first sentence is absolutely *wrong*. However, generally speaking, the corrected sentence (the second sentence) is preferable. We are calling the first sentence WEAK and the second sentence PREFERRED.

A.   WEAK: The examination was finished by all the students within the allocated time.
PREFERRED: *All the students finished the examination in time.*

B.   WEAK: The professor, who was tall and blond, lectured about medieval architecture.
PREFERRED: The *tall, blond* professor lectured about medieval architecture.

C.   WEAK: Paul read Jane's letter in an excited state of mind.
PREFERRED: Paul *excitedly* read Jane's letter.

D.   WEAK: The committee discussed the problem for a long time without being able to come to the point where a decision could be reached.
PREFERRED: The committee discussed the problem for a long time *without reaching a decision.*

E.   WEAK: Crime and illegal acts are on the rise.
PREFERRED: *Crime* is on the rise. (*Crime* is *illegal acts*.)

F.   WEAK: The girl who was wearing the colorful bathing suit is my cousin.
PREFERRED: The girl *wearing the colorful bathing suit* is my cousin.

G.   WEAK: The glass figurine that was on display in the store window appealed to me.
PREFERRED: The glass figurine *on display in the store window* appealed to me.

H. WEAK: Boston, which is the capital of Massachusetts, has many universities and colleges.

PREFERRED: Boston, *the capital of Massachusetts*, has many universities and colleges.

EXERCISE: Put "C" if the sentence seems correct as written. Put "W" if the sentence seems *wordy* (to have too many words).

_____1. The man indicated a negative response by shaking his head.

_____2. The house will probably be finished in four months.

_____3. The house on the corner burned down last night.

_____4. Jane went to the store with the purpose of selecting and purchasing a new dress.

_____5. Running on foot through the street, the thief was apprehended by the police.

_____6. My wife and I argued for hours before deciding to send our son to summer camp.

_____7. Bob saw several pieces of art that were expensive.

_____8. Jenny received several speeding tickets.

_____9. The ballerina danced her dances for hours.

_____10. Professor Blanton, who is the college president, will speak on this topic.

_____11. Betty opened the mysterious package cautiously.

_____12. The saleswoman in the red dress insulted me.

_____13. Three hours was the length of time that we found necessary to drive to New York.

_____14. The Louvre, a world-famous art museum, is in Paris, France.

_____15. The book was read by me in four hours.

Check your answers with the error key on page 210.

STYLE—SUBSTANDARD

Some words or phrases are *not* acceptable English.

1. *Ain't* should not be used as a negative form of *to be*.

    John *is not* here.

    I *am not* ready.

    They *are not* coming.

2. *Anywheres*, *nowheres*, *everywheres*, and *somewheres* are incorrect forms of *anywhere*, *nowhere*, *everywhere*, and *somewhere*.

    I cannot find him *anywhere*.

    Mary put her purse *somewhere*.

3. *Alright* is an incorrect form of *all right*.

    Do you feel *all right*?

4. *Kind of a* and *sort of a* are incorrect forms of *kind of* and *sort of*. (In other words, the *a* is unnecessary and incorrect.)

    That is a *kind of* plant that grows in Africa.

    John is the *sort of* man who worries about other people.

5. *Mad* should not be used to mean *angry*. (*Mad* means *insane*, *crazy*.)

    The teacher was very *angry* with John.

6. *Off of* is an incorrect form of *off*.

    The couple stepped *off* the bus.

7. *Suspicion* is a noun and cannot be used as a verb. The correct verb form is *suspect*.

    Mary *suspects* that her assistant may be stealing from her.

166

8. *The reason is because* is an incorrect form of *the reason is that*.

   The reason that John cannot attend the meeting *is that* he is sick.

9. *Is where* and *is when* are incorrect ways of defining the meaning of a word.

   "To imitate" means "to act the same way as someone else."

   A "cook-out" is "an outdoor party where food is generally cooked over charcoals."

10. *Different than* is an incorrect form of *different from*.

    John is *different from* his father.

ERROR EXAMPLES

A. WRONG: Betty ain't a good student.
   RIGHT: Betty *is not* a good student.

B. WRONG: The doctor looked everywheres for his prescription pad.
   RIGHT: The doctor looked *everywhere* for his prescription pad.

C. WRONG: The party was not wonderful, but at least the food was alright.
   RIGHT: The party was not wonderful, but at least the food was *all right*.

D. WRONG: That was the strangest kind of an animal that Harry had ever seen.
   RIGHT: That was the strangest *kind of* animal that Harry had ever seen.

E. WRONG: Sometimes a father can get very mad at his children.
   RIGHT: Sometimes a father can get very *angry with* his children.

F. WRONG: We try not to get off of the subject.
   RIGHT: We try not to get *off* the subject.

G. WRONG: The police suspicion that a local resident committed the crime.
   RIGHT: The police *suspect* that a local resident committed the crime.

H.   WRONG: The reason that Mary is so upset is because she lost her wallet.
     RIGHT: *The reason* that Mary is so upset *is that* she lost her wallet.

I.   WRONG: To "hyperventilate" is when one breathes too fast or too deeply.
     RIGHT: To "hyperventilate" is to "breathe too fast or too deeply."

J.   WRONG: California is different than Arizona.
     RIGHT: California is *different from* Arizona.

EXERCISE: Put "C" if the sentence is correct. Put "X" if substandard (unacceptable, incorrect) English is used.

_____1.   Most situations turn out all right in the long run.

_____2.   Gerald explained that the reason he was late was because he had had car trouble.

_____3.   A "loan-word" is "a word that has come from another language."

_____4.   The Smiths bought a kind of a car that gets good mileage.

_____5.   "Parallel" is when objects are an equal distance apart at every point.

_____6.   The vase was made of a sort of material found only in Australia.

_____7.   The children were nowheres to be found.

_____8.   Henry took the picture off the wall and put it away.

_____9.   It looked like a terrible accident, but everyone in the car was alright.

_____10. I believe the reason he left college was that he ran out of money.

_____11. The Browns ain't coming to the church meeting tonight.

_____12. I hope you do not suspicion that I cheated on the exam.

_____13. A "knock-out" is where a person is rendered unconscious by a blow.

_____14. The man acted so strangely that his family thought he was mad.

_____15. Good and bad people can be found anywheres in the world.

_____16. Do you find the United States much different than your country?

_____17.	The pen rolled off of the table and onto the floor.

_____18.	What sort of coat was the customer looking for?

_____19.	When John saw his grades, he felt very mad at his professor.

_____20.	What kind of a person could do a thing like this!

Check your answers with the error key on page 210.

STYLE—USAGE

Some words have similar meanings, but cannot be used interchangeably; that is, a choice must be made according to the grammatical situation.

1.	*Between/Among*

Between is used with *two* persons or things.

I cannot decide *between* these two blouses.

Among is used for *three or more* persons or things.

He was standing *among* several students.

2.	*Amount/Number*

Amount is used with *non-count nouns.*

NCN
He has a large *amount* of *money*.

Number is used with *count nouns.*

CN
She has a large *number* of *children*.

3.	*In/Into*

In is used with *non-motion* verbs.

He *is waiting in* the kitchen.

Into is used with verbs of *motion*.

He *ran into* the kitchen.

4. *Sit/Set*

Sit cannot take an object. *Sit* tells what a person or thing does for himself or by itself. The principal parts of *sit* are:

sit (simple form)	He *sits* by the window.
sat (past form)	Bob *sat* in his room and read.
sat (past participle)	The guests have already *sat* down.
sitting (present participle)	The vase is *sitting* on the table.

Set must have an object. *Set* tells what a person does for someone or something else. The principal parts of *set* are:

set (simple form)	OBJ. Do not *set* your *glass* on the piano.
set (past form)	OBJ. She *set* her *purse* on the floor last night.
set (past participle)	OBJ. Have you *set* the *table* yet?
setting (present participle)	OBJ. *Setting* the *vase* on the coffee table, Mary noticed that the vase had a crack in it.

5. *Lie/Lay*

Lie cannot take an object. *Lie* tells what a person or thing does for himself or by itself. The principal parts of *lie* are:

lie (simple form)	John *lies* on his bed for a few minutes after lunch every day.
lay (past form)	Mary *lay* on the sofa all yesterday afternoon.
lain (past participle)	The watch had *lain* unnoticed for several days before I found it.
lying (present participle)	A man was *lying* injured in the street after the accident.

Lay must have an object. *Lay* tells what a person or thing does for someone or something else. The principal parts of *lay* are:

lay (simple form)	OBJ. You should *lay* the *tiles* very evenly.

	OBJ.
laid (past form)	Mary *laid* her *son* on his bed early this afternoon.

	OBJ.
laid (past participle)	That hen has *laid* six *eggs* this week.

laying (present participle)	The workers are *laying* the

OBJ.
carpet now.

6. Rise/Raise

Rise cannot take an object. *Rise* tells what someone or something does for himself or by itself. The principal parts of *rise* are:

rise (simple form)	The temperature *rises* sharply in the afternoon.
rose (past form)	The sun *rose* at seven yesterday.
risen (past participle)	Prices have *risen* a great deal lately.
rising (present participle)	The baby's temperature is *rising* by the hour.

Raise must have an object. *Raise* tells what someone or something does for someone or something else. The principal parts of *raise* are:

	OBJ.
raise (simple form)	Please *raise* the *window* a little.

raised (past form)	The Browns *raised* their

OBJ.
children.

	OBJ.
raised (past participle)	The store has *raised* its *prices*.

raising (present participle)	The new book is *raising* many

OBJ.
interesting *questions*.

7. Learn/Teach

Learn is a verb which can be followed *directly* by an infinitive as an object.

INFIN.
She *learned to speak* French.

Teach is a verb which can be followed by an infinitive as an object. However, this infinitive must have its own subject. (See *Pronouns-Personal-Case*, page 109.)

      S   INFIN.
I *taught John to speak* French.

      S   INFIN.
I *taught him to speak* French.

8. Can/May

Can is a modal which means *ability*.

Mary *can* speak French.

John *can* play the piano.

May is a modal which means *permission*.

May I leave now?

John *may* have the last piece of cake.

9. Hanged/Hung

Hanged and *hung* are both correct past participle forms of the verb *hang*. BUT:

Hanged refers to *executions* (*killings*) of persons.

    PERSON
The *murderer* was *hanged* by the neck until dead.

Hung refers to *things*.

    THING
The *picture* was *hung* over the fireplace.

===============

ERROR EXAMPLES

A. WRONG: I believe we can handle this matter between the three of us.

    RIGHT: I believe we can handle this matter *among* the three of us.

B. WRONG: The students had a large amount of problems.

    RIGHT: The students had a large *number* of problems.

C. WRONG: The government has a large number of plutonium stored in a western state.
    RIGHT: The government has a large *amount* of plutonium stored in a western state.

D. WRONG: The frightened man rushed in the police station.
    RIGHT: The frightened man rushed *into* the police station.

E. WRONG: She sat her new chair between the sofa and the buffet.
    RIGHT: She *set* her new chair between the sofa and the buffet.

F. WRONG: Miss Jones learned us to swim in a few days.
    RIGHT: Miss Jones *taught* us to swim in a few days.

G. WRONG: Can I please have your attention?
    RIGHT: *May* I please have your attention?

H. WRONG: The clothes were neatly hanged on the clothesline.
    RIGHT: The clothes were neatly *hung* on the clothesline.

I. WRONG: The live wire laid in the street for hours after the storm.
    RIGHT: The live wire *lay* in the street for hours after the storm.

J. WRONG: Susan likes to lay down for a short nap every afternoon.
    RIGHT: Susan likes to *lie* down for a short nap every afternoon.

K. WRONG: We certainly hope that prices do not raise so quickly again.
    RIGHT: We certainly hope that prices do not *rise* so quickly again.

_____

EXERCISE: Put "C" if the sentence is correct. Put "X" if there is an error in usage.

_____1. The picture was hung over the fireplace.

_____2. That grandfather clock has sat in that same spot for forty years.

_____3. The volcano had lain dormant for fifty years when it suddenly erupted.

_____4. There was a surprising number of news coming from that country.

_____5. The bread dough has raised enough and is now ready to be baked.

_____6. The children's papers were hung about the classroom.

_____7. He distributed his wealth among his children, Betty and John.

_____8. Ellen can run faster than Beth.

_____9. They have already risen their family and are now free to travel.

_____10. A large amount of people showed up for the grand opening.

_____11. The jeweler has carefully set the diamond into a new mounting.

_____12. The harried student dashed quickly in the classroom.

_____13. When Betty arrived home, she found her husband laying on the sofa asleep as usual.

_____14. Parents usually feel proud when their baby learns to take his first few steps.

_____15. Children often ask if they can have candy.

_____16. The car suddenly left the road, slammed into a low wall, and turned over several times.

_____17. Never leave your purse lying where someone might be able to steal it.

_____18. The army had hanged several deserters in the weeks before the war finally ended.

_____19. John's father learned him to repair heavy equipment.

_____20. Mrs. Jones had carefully lain her children's clothes out ready for the children to put on.

Check your answers with the error key on page 211.

STYLE—WORDS OFTEN CONFUSED, GROUP I

The following words are often confused:

1. *Accept/Except*

Accept is a verb that means "to give a positive answer," or "to receive."

Susan *accepted* his offer of a job. (gave a positive answer)

The club *accepted* three new members. (received)

Except as a verb means "to exclude," "to keep out."

The boys *excepted* John from their club. (They did not accept him.)

Except is more commonly used as a preposition, meaning "with the exception of."

PREP.
Everybody *except* Jane went to the party. (Jane was *not* a member of the group that went to the party.)

2. *Advice/Advise*

Advise is a *verb*.

VERB
The doctor *advised* her to quit smoking.

Advice is a *noun*.

N
He gave me some good *advice*.

3. *All Ready/Already*

All ready is an *adjective phrase* meaning "completely ready."

ADJ. PHRASE
We were *all ready* to leave at eight o'clock.

Already is an *adverb* of time meaning "by or before a specific time."

ADV.
They had *already* left at five o'clock. (by five o'clock)

ADV.
He had *already* eaten when I arrived. (before I arrived)

4. *Altogether/All Together*

Altogether is an *adverb* meaning "completely."

ADV.
I am *altogether* tired.

All together is an *adjective phrase* meaning "in a group."

ADJ. PHRASE
The children are *all together* now and ready to go to the park.

5. *Beside/Besides*

>   The preposition *besides* means "except."

>>   Everyone *besides* John went to the party.

>   The preposition *beside* means "next to."

>>   John was standing *beside* me.   (NOT: *besides* me)

6. *Cloth/Clothes*

>   *Cloth* is a noun (usually used as a non-count noun) that means "material or fabric."

>>   NCN
>>   She bought some white *cloth* to make a wedding dress.

>   *Clothes* is a plural count noun meaning "garments used to cover the body."

>>   PL. CN
>>   She bought a lot of *clothes* when she was in Paris.

>>   PL. CN
>>   Beautiful *clothes* are usually expensive.

7. *Desert/Dessert*

>   A *desert* is "a dry area of the world with little vegetation."

>>   A large percentage of the world's surface is a *desert* where very little grows.

>   A *dessert* is "a sweet food usually eaten at the end of a meal."

>>   We had apple pie and ice cream for *dessert*.

8. *Differ From/Differ With*

>   *To differ from* is "to be dissimilar."

>>   Men *differ* physically *from* women.

>   *To differ with* is "to disagree with."

>>   I *differ with* you on this issue.   (I disagree with you.)

9. *Emigrate/Immigrate*

>*To emigrate* means "to leave one country to live in another."

>>In the early part of this century many people *emigrated* from Europe. They went to live in the United States.

>*To immigrate* means "to move *to* a new country."

>>In the early part of this century many people from Europe *immigrated* to the United States.

10. *Farther/Further*

>*Farther* means "to or at a more distant point in space."   (actual distance)

>>We have to drive a few miles *farther*.

>*Further* means "to or at a more distant point in time, degree, or quantity."   (figurative distance)

>>Let us consider this problem *further*.   (time)

>>We should do *further* research on this matter.   (quantity)

>>Be careful not to excite the children *further*.   (degree)

ERROR EXAMPLES

A. WRONG: John did not except my invitation to the party.
    RIGHT: John did not *accept* my invitation to the party.

B. WRONG: You will find your umbrella besides the table.
    RIGHT: You will find your umbrella *beside* the table.

C. WRONG: Please advice him that he must hurry.
    RIGHT: Please *advise* him that he must hurry.

D. WRONG: Susan gave Paul some excellent advise.
    RIGHT: Susan gave Paul some excellent *advice*.

E. WRONG: Please ask the students not to stand altogether in the hall.
    RIGHT: Please ask the students not to stand *all together* in the hall.

F. WRONG: I am all together disgusted with his behavior.
    RIGHT: I am *altogether* disgusted with his behavior.

G. WRONG: Has John really finished his homework all ready?
    RIGHT: Has John really finished his homework *already*?

H.   WRONG: Dinner is already to be served.
     RIGHT: Dinner is *all ready* to be served.

I.   WRONG: Mary bought new cloth to wear to the party.
     RIGHT: Mary bought new *clothes* to wear to the party.

J.   WRONG: Be careful to take lots of water when you cross the dessert.
     RIGHT: Be careful to take lots of water when you cross the *desert*.

K.   WRONG: Would you like a piece of cake for desert?
     RIGHT: Would you like a piece of cake for *dessert*?

L.   WRONG: New York differs with Washington, DC.
     RIGHT: New York differs *from* Washington, DC.

M.   WRONG: When discussing politics, Bob frequently differs from his father.
     RIGHT: When discussing politics, Bob frequently differs *with* his father.

N.   WRONG: During times of economic hardship people may have to immigrate from their native land.
     RIGHT: During times of economic hardship people may have to *emigrate* from their native land.

O.   WRONG: I believe Martha's house is further down the road.
     RIGHT: I believe Martha's house is *farther* down the road.

P.   WRONG: Do you feel it is necessary to think about this matter farther?
     RIGHT: Do you feel it is necessary to think about this matter *further*?

EXERCISE: Put "C" if the sentence is correct. Put "X" if there is an error in word choice.

_____1.   He has all ready spent next month's allowance.

_____2.   Mary looked all day for clothes suitable to cover the worn pillows.

_____3.   Will John take his doctor's advice?

_____4.   In a surprise vote the board excepted John from membership.

_____5.   Can you get everybody altogether for the meeting in ten minutes?

_____6.   Helen enjoys wearing the clothes she designs.

_____7. The two political candidates certainly differed loudly from each other.

_____8. One reason people will emigrate from their country is to escape political persecution.

_____9. Did you look besides the sofa for your book?

_____10. Do not try to drive further today.

_____11. Will you accept my apologies?

_____12. Why did so many people immigrate from Uruguay to go to Australia?

_____13. I was surprised at the advise he gave me.

_____14. Steve differs with his father in physical appearance.

_____15. Let me give you some farther instruction.

Check your answers with the error key on page 212.

STYLE—WORDS OFTEN CONFUSED, GROUP II

The following words are often confused:

1. *Formally/Formerly*

    Formally means "in a formal way."

    The meeting was conducted very *formally*.

    Formerly means "previously," "at an earlier time."

    June was *formerly* a member of that club.

2. *Healthful/Healthy*

    Healthful means "good for one's health."

    Vegetables are *healthful* foods.

    Healthy means "in a good condition of health."

    All of his children are *healthy*.

3. *Illusion/Allusion*

An *illusion* is "a false idea" or "unreal image."

The magician created the *illusion* that he was flying through the air.

An *allusion* is "an indirect reference."

The professor made an *allusion* to Greek mythology.

4. *Imply/Infer*

To imply is "to suggest without stating directly." Only the speaker or writer can *imply*.

Susan *implied* that she was not happy with her job.

To infer is "to make a conclusion based on evidence not directly stated." Only the listener or reader can *infer*.

I *inferred* from her letter that Susan was not happy with her job.

5. *Its/It's*

Its is the singular possessive pronoun for things.

PRON.
The tree lost *its* leaves when the weather turned cold.

It's is the contraction for *it is*.

It's a nice day today. (*It is* a nice day today.)

6. *Leave/Let*

To leave means "to go away from."

He *leaves* school at three o'clock every day.

To let means "to permit."

John *let* me borrow his car.

7. *Loose/Lose*

The adjective *loose* means "not tight."

ADJ.
This blouse is too *loose*. I need a smaller size.

To lose is a verb meaning "to leave behind by accident" or "to cease having unintentionally."

VERB
I often *lose* my car keys.

8. Most/Almost

The adjective *most* is the superlative form of *many*, meaning "the largest number."

ADJ.
Most people like ice cream.

The adjective *most* is also the superlative form of *much*, meaning "the largest amount."

ADJ.
Most coffee comes from Brazil.

Almost is an adverb meaning "slightly less than," "not quite," or "very nearly."

ADV.
Almost all the students are here.

ADV.
He is *almost* ready to leave.

ADV.
He *almost* won the race.

9. Plane/Plain

The noun *plane* often means "airplane."

N
His *plane* will arrive in Chicago at nine o'clock.

The adjective *plain* means "simple," "not fancy," or "undecorated."

ADJ.
Her dress was very *plain*.

10. Principal/Principle

The adjective *principal* means "chief" or "very important." The noun *principal* means "chief official."

ADJ.
The *principal* reason for his failure was his lack of interest in his job.

He wants to talk to the *principal* of the school. [N appears above *principal*]

The noun *principle* means "fundamental truth."

He is studying the *principles* of accounting. [N appears above *principles*]

11. *Quiet/Quite*

Quiet is an adjective meaning "not noisy."

It was a very *quiet* party. [ADJ. appears above *quiet*]

Quite is an adverb meaning "completely" or "to a degree."

He is *quite* nervous today. [ADV. appears above *quite*]

He is *quite* tall. [ADV. appears above *quite*]

ERROR EXAMPLES

A. **WRONG:** He spoke formerly and eloquently on that serious subject.
   RIGHT: He spoke *formally* and eloquently on that serious subject.

B. **WRONG:** John was formally a member of that club, but he resigned.
   RIGHT: John was *formerly* a member of that club, but he resigned.

C. **WRONG:** Fruit is a very healthy food.
   RIGHT: Fruit is a very *healthful* food.

D. **WRONG:** The politician made a clever illusion to the political problems his chief rival was having.
   RIGHT: The politician made a clever *allusion* to the political problems his chief rival was having.

E. **WRONG:** Mary never said it directly, but she inferred that she did not like me.
   RIGHT: Mary never said it directly, but she *implied* that she did not like me.

F. **WRONG:** Would you please leave me do this job by myself.
   RIGHT: Would you please *let* me do this job by myself.

G.   WRONG: Linda cannot wear this belt because it is too lose.
     RIGHT: Linda cannot wear this belt because it is too *loose*.

H.   WRONG: Did you loose your watch?
     RIGHT: Did you *lose* your watch?

I.   WRONG: Most everybody who is supposed to come is here
              already.
     RIGHT: *Almost* everybody who is supposed to come is here
              already.

J.   WRONG: Which plain are you taking to New York?
     RIGHT: Which *plane* are you taking to New York?

K.   WRONG: The principle of my daughter's school was educated
              in Europe.
     RIGHT: The *principal* of my daughter's school was educated
              in Europe.

L.   WRONG: We spent a quite evening at home together.
     RIGHT: We spent a *quiet* evening at home together.

M.   WRONG: The ship lost it's way from Florida to Bimini.
     RIGHT: The ship lost *its* way from Florida to Bimini.

EXERCISE: Put "C" if the sentence is correct. Put "X" if there is
an error in word choice.

_____1.   Do you think that its difficult to learn a foreign language?

_____2.   The modern art piece they chose was plain but bold.

_____3.   The principle fact I would like you to remember concerns
            the human personality.

_____4.   Are you quite sure you wish to spend that much for one
            chair?

_____5.   His wife was formerly married to the Spanish Ambassador.

_____6.   Her parents are quite old, but relatively healthful.

_____7.   The young actress was able to create the allusion that she
            was middle-aged.

_____8.   From reading his letter, I inferred that he was having finan-
            cial problems.

_____9.   He put his keys in his coat pocket so that he would not
            loose them.

_____10. Can you let the student continue with this course if he
            makes up all missed work?

_____11. Please leave him find out the truth by himself.

_____12. I do not trust that man; he has absolutely no principles.

_____13. I most fell off my seat laughing when I saw the clown chase the bull.

_____14. I think my battery has a loose connection.

_____15. Are you trying to infer that I should study more?

Check your answers with the error key on page 212.

STYLE—WORDS OFTEN CONFUSED, GROUP III

The following words are often confused:

1. *Respectfully/Respectively*

    Respectfully means "with respect."

    > The audience rose *respectfully* when the President entered.

    Respectively means "in the order given."

    > The Thompsons lived in Chicago, Los Angeles, and New York *respectively*.

2. *So/So That*

    So is a conjunction joining a clause of *result* to a main clause.

    > It rained a lot that year, *so* there were lots of wildflowers to enjoy.   (*result*)

    So that joins a clause of *purpose* to a main clause.

    > We wore raincoats *so that* we would not get our clothes wet.   (*purpose*)

3. *Stationary/Stationery*

Stationary means "in a fixed position."

The only time most children are *stationary* is when they are asleep.

Stationery refers to writing supplies.

That *stationery* store sells fancy writing paper and envelopes.

4. *Their/There/They're*

Their is the third-person plural possessive pronoun.

PRON.
They sold *their* home to a couple from London.

There is (1) an adverb of place or (2) an expletive that tells of existence.

ADV.
Your package is *there* on the counter.

EXPLETIVE
There are fifty states in the United States.

They're is the contraction of *they are*.

They're ready to see you now.

5. *To/Too/Two* (See also *Modifiers—Too, Very*, and *Enough*, page 52).

To is (1) part of the infinitive form or (2) a preposition.

INFIN.
I like *to walk* in the rain.

PREP.
I walked *to* the store.

Too is an adverb indicating an excess.

ADV.
It is *too* hot today to study.

Two is a number (2).

I have *two* children, John and Greg.

6. *Weather/Whether*

Weather is a noun meaning "atmospheric conditions."

N
It is nice *weather* today for a picnic.

Whether is a conjunction meaning "if."

CONJ.
I do not know *whether* he will come to the party.

Who's/Whose

Who's is the contraction for *who is*.

I do not know *who's* coming tonight.

Whose is (1) a question word or (2) a possessive relative pronoun.

QW
Whose book is this?

PRON.
I met the man *whose* daughter is in my class.

ERROR EXAMPLES

A. WRONG: Last summer I visited the capital cities of Connecticut, Massachusetts, and Rhode Island respectfully.
    RIGHT: Last summer I visited the capital cities of Connecticut, Massachusetts, and Rhode Island *respectively*.

B. WRONG: I bought a car so I would not have to walk to work.
    RIGHT: I bought a car *so that* I would not have to walk to work.

C. WRONG: A model must sometimes remain stationery for hours at a time.
    RIGHT: A model must sometimes remain *stationary* for hours at a time.

D. WRONG: Please put the piano over their near the window.
    RIGHT: Please put the piano over *there* near the window.

E. WRONG: Robin is really much to nervous to be in public relations.
    RIGHT: Robin is really much *too* nervous to be in public relations.

F.   WRONG: Bob is not sure weather or not he will be able to attend your opening next week.

     RIGHT: Bob is not sure *whether* or not he will be able to attend your opening next week.

G.   WRONG: Who's purse do you think this is?

     RIGHT: *Whose* purse do you think this is?

EXERCISE: Put "C" if the sentence is correct. Put "X" if there is an error in word choice.

_____1.   The whether is usually nice in Hawaii all year round.

_____2.   They're buying a home in the city next year.

_____3.   We met two of my father's business associates at the dinner.

_____4.   Did you find out whose coming early?

_____5.   I love to browse in stationary stores.

_____6.   Bob thinks this material is too difficult for first-year students.

_____7.   The students left there books on the floor during the exam.

_____8.   The audience applauded respectively at the end of her speech.

_____9.   Do not send any of these booklets too people who did not put their complete address on the form.

_____10. He parked his car on the street so that he would not have to pay for parking in the garage.

Check your answers with the error key on page 213.

STYLE—CORRELATIVE CONJUNCTIONS

The following is a list of *Correlative Conjunctions*. Remember that they are always used in these pairs. Do not mix them up.

both...and
either...or
neither...nor
not only...but also
whether...or

That music is *both* disturbing *and* loud.

Either he is going to get a job here *or* he is going to study in Los Angeles.

He is *neither* well qualified *nor* sufficiently experienced for that position.

He refused to say *whether* he would come to the meeting in person *or* send a representative.

That horse is *not only* the youngest one in the race *but also* the only one to win two years in a row.

NOTES:

    a.   Do not use *both . . . and* for three or more nouns or adjectives.

        Mary, Blair, and Margie are going to arrive late.

OR

        Mary and Blair, as well as Margie, are going to arrive late.

    b.   *Whether* may sometimes be used alone.

        I do not know *whether* she received the package.

ERROR EXAMPLES

A. **WRONG:** Both John, Ernest, and Paul are going to the game.
     RIGHT: John *and* Ernest, *as well as* Paul, are going to the game.

OR

    John, Ernest, and Paul are going to the game.

B. **WRONG:** That book includes only not records but also cassettes.
     RIGHT: That book includes *not only* records *but also* cassettes.

C. **WRONG:** She won the dance competition because she had both originality as well as grace.
     RIGHT: She won the dance competition because she had *both* originality *and* grace.

D. **WRONG:** She decided not only to start a diet, but to join an exercise class also.
     RIGHT: She decided *not only* to start a diet, *but also* to join an exercise class.

E. **WRONG:** That coin is not only valuable but rare also.
     RIGHT: That coin is *not only* valuable *but also* rare.

F. WRONG: Neither the public or private sector of the economy
            will be seriously affected by this new regulation.
    RIGHT: Neither the public *nor* private sector of the economy
            will be seriously affected by this new regulation.

G. WRONG: He refused to work either in Chicago nor in Detroit.
    RIGHT: He refused to work *either* in Chicago *or* in Detroit.

EXERCISE: Put "C" if the sentence is correct. Put "X" if there is a correlative conjunction error.

_____1. Some students can neither write or speak accurately.

_____2. That course includes not only TOEFL preparation but also techniques of test-taking.

_____3. They like both living abroad as well as living at home.

_____4. Tom won not only the 100-yard dash but the broad jump also.

_____5. He is neither limber nor quick.

_____6. Either you will attend class regularly or you can expect a low grade.

_____7. Whether out of necessity or greed, he accepted the bribe.

_____8. Both the president and the vice-president gave speeches last night.

_____9. The play was both long, boring, and depressing.

_____10. He is both deceptive as well as irresponsible.

Check your answers with the error key on page 213.

===

STYLE—SUBJECT/VERB AGREEMENT

===

Singular subjects take singular verbs. Plural subjects take plural verbs.

              S   VERB
The *secretary* in this office *comes* to work at eight.

              S   VERB
The *secretaries* in this office *come* to work at eight.

Problems in determining the subject:

1. Subjects are never found in prepositional phrases.

    S   PREP. PHRASE   VERB
    The *price of all these items is* twenty dollars.

    S   PREP. PHRASE VERB
    The *characters in this story are* well developed.

2. *Here* and *there* are not subjects. Look *after* the verb to find the subject.

    VERB   S
    Here *comes* the *bus.*

    VERB   S
    There *are* many good *reasons* to study language.

3. The subject also follows the verb in this pattern:

    ADV.   VERB   S
    On the door *was* a *wreath* of flowers.

    ADV.   VERB   S
    Around the corner *are* several small *shops.*

4. Expressions introduced with words such as *along with, besides, like, as well as,* and *including* do not change the number of the subject.

    S   VERB
    Mr. *Jones* , along with his wife and six children, *is going* to Paris.

    S   VERB
    The *weather* , as well as economic conditions, *is* a consideration

    S   VERB
    Several *candidates* , including John Baker, *are going.*

5. When two subjects are joined by *either . . . or* or *neither . . . nor*, the subject closer to the verb determines its number.

    S   S   VERB
    Neither *Mary* nor her *sisters are going* to the party.

    S   S   VERB
    Either my *sisters* or my *mother is going* to the wedding.

6. Some words look plural but are singular. Among these words are *economics, mathematics, physics, news,* and *politics.*

    S   VERB
    The *news was* good.

S   VERB
Mathematics is a challenging field.

7. The subject of a relative clause, *who*, *which*, or *that*, is singular or plural depending on its *antecedent*.

ANTE-
CEDENT   S   VERB
The *students who come* to class every day generally progress rapidly.

ANTE-
CEDENT   S   VERB
Bob is one of my *friends who are helping* me paint my house.

ANTE-
CEDENT   S   VERB
Bob is the only *one* of my friends *who is helping* me paint my house.

==

ERROR EXAMPLES

A. WRONG: His influence over the last ten years have grown considerably.
    RIGHT: His influence over the last ten years *has* grown considerably.

B. WRONG: Over the fireplace hangs several small paintings.
    RIGHT: Over the fireplace *hang* several small paintings.

C. WRONG: Neither the moon nor the stars is visible.
    RIGHT: Neither the moon nor the stars *are* visible.

D. WRONG: A study of all possible causes of these multiple fractures are in order.
    RIGHT: A study of all possible causes of these multiple fractures *is* in order.

E. WRONG: There occurs to me a few possible explanations for his behavior.
    RIGHT: There *occur* to me a few possible explanations for his behavior.

F. WRONG: His furniture, including a dining room table and six chairs, are being sold.
    RIGHT: His furniture, including a dining room table and six chairs, *is* being sold.

G. WRONG: I asked all the students who was willing to help to meet me at the school.
    RIGHT: I asked all the students who *were* willing to help to meet me at the school.

H. WRONG: The college newspaper prints only the news that are of interest to the students and faculty.
    RIGHT: The college newspaper prints only the news that *is* of interest to the students and faculty.

I. WRONG: Either the students or the teacher were mistaken.
    RIGHT: Either the students or the teacher *was* mistaken.

EXERCISE: Put "C" if the sentence is correct. Put "X" if there is an error in subject-verb agreement.

_____1. There are several jobs available.

_____2. Along the beach was several small boats that had been washed ashore.

_____3. Neither my sisters nor my brother is ready to begin college.

_____4. The lack of logic in his arguments never cease to surprise me.

_____5. She was determined to study nuclear physics, which was the most difficult course offered at that school.

_____6. Students who have difficulty with this subject should try to find someone who is willing to tutor them.

_____7. Either her husband or her children is going to be upset no matter what decision she makes.

_____8. Betty is one of the women who is responsible for writing that.

_____9. My uncle, as well as my father, are going to Canada on business.

_____10. The only one of his friends who is upset with John is Bob.

Check your answers with the error key on page 214.

STYLE—PARTS OF SPEECH*

Sometimes a word can be identified as a noun, adjective, adverb, or verb by its suffix (ending).

1. The following suffixes usually indicate *nouns*:

-ion, -sion, -tion	popula*tion*
-acy	accura*cy*
-age	im*age*
-ance, -ence	perman*ence*
-hood	child*hood*
-ar, -or	schol*ar*, doct*or*
-ism	social*ism*
-ist	art*ist*
-ment	govern*ment*
-ness	happi*ness*
-y	beaut*y*
-ty	reali*ty*, capaci*ty*

2. The following suffixes usually indicate *adjectives:*

-al	natur*al*
-ful	beauti*ful*
-ly	friend*ly*
-ic	chron*ic*
-ish	child*ish*
-like	child*like*
-ous	popul*ous*, numer*ous*
-y	happ*y*
-ate	accur*ate*
-able, -ible	cap*able*, terr*ible*

3. The following suffix usually indicates *adverbs:*

-ly	happi*ly*, readi*ly*, beautiful*ly*

*See also *Modifiers—Adjective/Adverb Confusion*, page 27.

4. The following suffixes usually indicate *verbs*:

-ify	beaut*ify*
-ate	popul*ate*
-ize	rea*lize*

NOTE:

There are some exceptions to these general rules.

ERROR EXAMPLES

A. WRONG: I was amazed at her natural beautiful.
      RIGHT: I was amazed at her natural *beauty*.

B. WRONG: His illness was chronically.
      RIGHT: His illness was *chronic*.

C. WRONG: Happily is a rare state of being.
      RIGHT: *Happiness* is a rare state of being.

D. WRONG: He had an unhappy childlike.
      RIGHT: He had an unhappy *childhood*.

E. WRONG: You should reality the truth.
      RIGHT: You should *realize* the truth.

F. WRONG: That country has a very large populate.
      RIGHT: That country has a very large *population*.

EXERCISE: Put "C" if the sentence is correct. Put "X" if there is an error in the part of speech according to the suffix.

_____1.   Bob hopes to beauty his home by painting and carpeting.

_____2.   Lawrence is a very happily man.

_____3.   Japan is a very populous nation.

_____4.   What do you think is the real of that situation?

_____5.   Her manner was friendly and natural.

_____6.   Dr. Smith's capacity for hard work was incredible.

_____7.   I never questioned his accurately.

_____8.   Jane was surprised that he spoke so childish.

_____9. That new medicine will not be readily available until next year.

_____10. Does the book list the populous of that country in 1950?

Check your answers with the error key on page 214.

STYLE—PREPOSITIONS
(GENERAL USE)

A preposition is generally used to show the relationship between its object and other words in the sentence. The kinds of relationships which can be shown are as follows:

1. Place (*in*, *on*, *under*, *over*, etc.)

    Your book is *in* the desk drawer.

2. Direction (*to*, *toward*, *into*, etc.)

    The student ran *into* the room.

3. Time (*in*, *on*, *at*, etc.)

    We can meet *at* three o'clock.

4. Agent (*by*)

    This book was written *by* an elderly woman.

5. Instrument (*by*, *with*)

    I heard the news *by* telephone.   (*communication*)

    She came *by* plane.   (*transportation*)

    He opened the door *with* a key.   (*instrument*; *tool*)

    Note: Use *by* + N (no article) for *communication* and *transportation*.
    Examples: *by phone*, *by radio*, *by telegram* and *by train*, *by car*, *by boat*

6. Accompaniment (*with*)

They like spaghetti *with* red sauce.

Mrs. Jones went to the bank *with* her husband.

7. Purpose (*for*) (See also *Basic Patterns—To/For* [*Purpose*]), page 140.

He went to the store *for* bread.

Note: Never use *for* + *V* + *ing* to express the purpose of the verb.
Example: He went to the store <u>for buying</u> bread.
                                      WRONG

8. Partition/Possession (*of*)

They painted the front *of* the building.

He broke the top *of* the table.

9. Measure (*by, of*)

We buy our rice *by* the pound.

Please buy a quart *of* milk.

10. Similarity (*like*)

John looks *like* his father.

11. Capacity (*as*)

Bill worked *as* a lifeguard this summer.

ERROR EXAMPLES

A. WRONG: We damaged the front to the car.
    RIGHT: We damaged the front *of* the car.

B. WRONG: That store sells flour for the 25-pound sack.
    RIGHT: That store sells flour *by* the 25-pound sack.

C. WRONG: Betty worked like a secretary for a few months.
    RIGHT: Betty worked *as* a secretary for a few months.

D. WRONG: For dinner we had chicken by rice.
    RIGHT: For dinner we had chicken *with* rice.

E. WRONG: Your son is waiting for you to his office.
    RIGHT: Your son is waiting for you *in* his office.

F.   WRONG: The next performance begins in sundown.
     RIGHT: The next performance begins *at* sundown.

G.   WRONG: We went to the bank to money.
     RIGHT: We went to the bank *for* money.

H.   WRONG: These artifacts are made with Indians living in Peru.
     RIGHT: These artifacts are made *by* Indians living in Peru.

I.   WRONG: Jane went for Chicago with train.
     RIGHT: Jane went *to* Chicago *by* train.

J.   WRONG: Susan sings as her mother.
     RIGHT: Susan sings *like* her mother.

EXERCISE: Put "C" if the sentence is correct. Put "X" if there is an error with the preposition.

_____1.   We drove the car into the driveway.

_____2.   They came to visit us with a car.

_____3.   The movie was reviewed by the critic.

_____4.   He came to the United States for an education.

_____5.   Did you notice that Bob walks as his father?

_____6.   He opened the door by key.

_____7.   Paula looks nothing like her sister.

_____8.   They purchased the material for the yard.

_____9.   Barbara enjoyed working as a bank teller for one summer.

_____10. He went to the store for buying a newspaper.

_____11. We would like to invite you to our home for dinner on your birthday.

_____12. He did not notice that the leg for the chair was broken before he sat down.

_____13. John went to the store to buy two pounds butter.

_____14. Would you please bring us some coffee with our meal.

_____15. They met at the movies 7:00.

Check your answers with the error key on page 215.

Check your answers with the error key on page 215.

STYLE—PREPOSITIONS IN COMBINATIONS

1. The following *verb plus preposition* combinations always appear as follows and must be learned together:

agree on (something)	We *agree on* that point.
agree with (a person)	I *agree with* you on that matter.
approve of	Betty *approves of* exercising.
arrive at OR in	They *arrived in* Tokyo last night.
complain about	Please do not *complain about* the prices.
consent to	She *consented to* her daughter's marriage.
comment on	She *commented on* his new suit.
consist of	Water *consists of* hydrogen and oxygen.
depend on	I am *depending on* good weather for my party.
laugh at	We *laughed at* his silly behavior.
object to	Do you *object to* my smoking?
succeed in	He *succeeded in* making everyone angry.

Note: The correct verb form to use after a preposition is a *gerund* (*V + ing*). See *Verbs—Verbals,* rule 3, page 87.

2. Some other *verb plus preposition* combinations take two objects.

compare . . . with OR to	Do not *compare* me *with* (OR *to*) my sister.
excuse . . . for	I cannot *excuse* you *for* being late.
prefer . . . to	She *prefers* coffee *to* tea.
remind . . . of	He *reminded* me *of* my appointment.
thank . . . for	I *thanked* him *for* letting me use his car.

3. There are many *adjective plus preposition* combinations that occur with the verb *to be*.

be afraid of	Henry *is afraid of* dogs.
be accustomed to	I *was accustomed to* seeing him every day.

198

be aware of	*Are* you *aware of* his problem?
be bored with	Jane *is bored with* school.
be certain of	You cannot *be certain of* the date.
be disappointed with	Susan *was disappointed with* that restaurant.
be familiar with	*Is* Doctor Jones *familiar with* that new technique?
be famous for	Wisconsin *is famous for* its cheese.
be frightened by	Do not *be frightened by* the thunder and lightning.
be happy with	The Joneses *are* very *happy with* their new home.
be in favor of	*Are* you *in favor of* women's liberation?
be interested in	John *is interested in* attending a large university.
be opposed to	He *is* really *opposed to* buying a new car.
be satisfied with	He *is* not *satisfied with* his new radio.
be surprised at OR by	Do not *be surprised at* his behavior.
be tired of	Maria *is* very *tired of* working six days a week.
be worried about	Mark *is* very *worried about* his sick child.

4. Some prepositions exist in fixed phrases.

according to	*According to* the news, the government has fallen.
along with	Can you take this package, *along with* these letters, to the post office?
as well as	I enjoy art *as well as* history.
because of	*Because of* the rain, there will be no picnic.
by means of	The thief entered the house *by means of* an open window.
by way of	John went to Paris *by way of* London.
in addition to	*In addition to* going to school full-time, Patricia works part-time.
in case of	*In case of* fire, pull this alarm.
in consideration of	*In consideration of* all your help, I would like to take you to dinner.
in contrast to OR with	*In contrast to* last summer, this summer is cool.
in deference to	*In deference to* his age, we did not argue with him.

in hopes of	We came here *in hopes of* meeting the president.
in lieu of	He gave an oral report *in lieu of* a written report.
in pursuit of	The police were *in pursuit of* the thief.
in search of	They went into the mountains *in search of* gold.
in spite of	*In spite of* his good intentions, he did not study very much.
in the face of	*In the face of* a severe drought, the tribe moved to a new location.
in terms of	He was a good husband *in terms of* earning a good living.

ERROR EXAMPLES

A. **WRONG:**   Is John familiar enough for this part of town to find your house?
   RIGHT: Is John familiar enough *with* this part of town to find your house?

B. **WRONG:**   In spite the rain, the party has not been canceled.
   RIGHT: In spite *of* the rain, the party has not been canceled.

C. **WRONG:**   My son was surprised with his teacher's decision.
   RIGHT: My son was surprised *at* (OR *by*) his teacher's decision.

D. **WRONG:**   He continued to work in the face to his doctor's disapproval.
   RIGHT: He continued to work in the face *of* his doctor's disapproval.

E. **WRONG:**   Clyde is bored for living in the country.
   RIGHT: Clyde is bored *with* living in the country.

F. **WRONG:**   Bob is always complaining for the heat in Arizona in the summertime.
   RIGHT: Bob is always complaining *about* the heat in Arizona in the summertime.

G. **WRONG:**   How do you think Rome compares by Paris?
   RIGHT: How do you think Rome compares *to* Paris?

H. **WRONG:**   Veronica is tired by waiting for me to get ready.
   RIGHT: Veronica is tired *of* waiting for me to get ready.

I. **WRONG:**   Do you object with my cutting some of your flowers?
   RIGHT: Do you object *to* my cutting some of your flowers?

J. WRONG: Do you think it is fair to excuse him by being late?
    RIGHT: Do you think it is fair to excuse him *for* being late?

K. WRONG: Betty reminds me to my sister.
    RIGHT: Betty reminds me *of* my sister.

L. WRONG: Who is in favor for adjourning the meeting early?
    RIGHT: Who is in favor *of* adjourning the meeting early?

M. WRONG: What time do you think you will arrive to London?
    RIGHT: What time do you think you will arrive *in* London?

N. WRONG: He asked if he could paint the apartment in lieu for a month's rent.
    RIGHT: He asked if he could paint the apartment in lieu *of* a month's rent.

O. WRONG: One cannot depend with luck to bring success.
    RIGHT: One cannot depend *on* luck to bring success.

P. WRONG: He studied art in addition with his regular course of studies.
    RIGHT: He studied art in addition *to* his regular course of studies.

Q. WRONG: George is not accustomed at speaking in public.
    RIGHT: George is not accustomed *to* speaking in public.

R. WRONG: Clyde is quite satisfied by his new apartment.
    RIGHT: Clyde is quite satisfied *with* his new apartment.

S. WRONG: Can we agree with a date for our next meeting?
    RIGHT: Can we agree *on* a date for our next meeting?

EXERCISE: Put "C" if the sentence is correct. Put "X" if there is an error with the preposition.

_____1. Did you agree to your father on which car you should buy?

_____2. They arrived to Paris sometime early in the summer.

_____3. Were the students accustomed to leaving early on Fridays?

_____4. Whether we leave early or late depends about your schedule.

_____5. The doctor objected to the patient's leaving the hospital a day early.

_____6. David was surprised at the amount of time necessary to fix the car.

_____7. Henry was not very satisfied with the lab report that he wrote.

_____8. Switzerland is famous of its beautiful mountains.

_____9. The soldier showed great courage in the face of death.

_____10. This home certainly does not compare favorably at our old one.

_____11. The committee was in favor of increasing his salary.

_____12. Were you tired with waiting for her to call?

_____13. He did not expect us to comment to his newly decorated office.

_____14. Are you familiar to early American art?

_____15. He spent his life in search for absolute truth.

Check your answers with the error key on page 215.

CHAPTER QUIZ—Style

DIRECTIONS: Write the letter of the word or phrase that best completes the following sentences.

_____1. The young couple liked to buy, redecorate, and _____ _____ older homes for a profit.

(A) resold
(B) reselling
(C) resell
(D) to resell

_____2. The management was shocked to realize that its trusted employee was _____ of stealing a large sum of money from the company.

(A) suspicioned
(B) suspicioning
(C) suspected
(D) suspicion

_____3. Not only having graduated *magna cum laude* _____ _____, Steve made his family very proud of him.

(A) and also having finished first in the national competition
(B) also having finished first in the national competition
(C) but having finished first in the national competition
(D) but also having finished first in the national competition

_____4. _____ his earlier study, Dr. Melon's new study indicates a general warming trend in global weather.

(A) In contrast of
(B) In contrast to
(C) In contrast by
(D) In contrast as

_____5. The workers have finished pouring the floors, and _____ _____ waiting for the house to be framed.

(A) there
(B) they're
(C) their
(D) they

_____6. The reason he wants to take a leave of absence is
_____.

(A) because he is needing a complete rest
(B) because he needs a complete rest
(C) that he needs a complete rest
(D) because a complete rest is needed by him

_____7. The teacher objected to the students' _____
their opened umbrellas near the door.

(A) sitting
(B) having sat
(C) setting
(D) sat

_____8. He was a dynamic figure who inspired awe, devotion, and
_____ in his followers.

(A) love
(B) loving feelings
(C) feelings of love
(D) loveliness

_____9. The rich young newlyweds bought a beautiful new home
and _____.

(A) their pool was installed
(B) had a pool installed
(C) had a pool being installed
(D) a pool was installed

_____10. My boss _____ my taking two weeks' leave
without pay.

(A) consented to
(B) consented for
(C) consented of
(D) consented about

_____11. The students worked on the problem for several minutes
before _____.

(A) they came to the realization that this problem was one
that had no solution
(B) realizing that it was insolvable
(C) they were able to understand that this problem which
seemed merely difficult was, in reality, insolvable
(D) the insolvability of the problem was realized by them

_____12. Henry went to the conference _____ about government contracts.

    (A) to learn
    (B) with the purpose of learning
    (C) in order to have the opportunity to learn
    (D) in order to be in a position to learn

_____13. Try as he might, he could never manage to get an _____ balance in his checkbook.

    (A) accuracy
    (B) accurately
    (C) accurate
    (D) accurateness

_____14. The professor asked the students _____.

    (A) not only to write a report or give a speech
    (B) either to write a report or give a speech
    (C) neither to write a report or give a speech
    (D) neither to write a report but give a speech

_____15. She writes such _____ poetry that it is hard to believe she has never had a formal education.

    (A) beauty
    (B) beautiful
    (C) beautifully
    (D) beautify

DIRECTIONS: Write the letter of the *incorrect* part of the sentence in the space provided.

_____1. The design <u>for</u> the new community center <u>combines</u> both
          A   B

refreshing originality <u>as well as</u> an impressive respect for
                   C

the traditional architecture <u>of</u> the area.
                       D

_____2. He described his best friend as <u>being</u> adventuresome, <u>witty</u>,
                           A   B

<u>and</u> successful, but very <u>plane-looking.</u>
 C   D

_____3.   In order to earn enough money to complete his educa-
            A

tion, John worked last summer like a lifeguard at a girls'
                                    B   C   D

camp.

_____4.   When I was at the grocery store, I realized that the prices
            A   B

of many items had been rised.
C   D

_____5.   The natives of that region gathered plants and hunted small
                        A

animals, but supplies were bought by them in the market-
              B   C

place, which they visited infrequently.
                          D

_____6.   Our trek in the Sahara Dessert was extremely fascinating,
                A   B   C

totally challenging, and enormously relaxing.
                                    D

_____7.   The political polls indicated that most people were not as
                                            A   B

much in favor with the new law as was previously thought.
              C   D

_____8.   We did not hire him because his only experience was
                                A   B

coaching a high school basketball team, leading a

parochial school choir, and to work as a substitute teacher.
C   D

_____9.   The new teacher was both surprised and delighted when
                                A   B

she realized that her class consisted with many students
                                        C

from faraway countries.
     D

_____10. According to my calculations, the cost of two dozen roses

are fifty dollars, which is considerably less than
A   B

the sixty-two dollars I was charged.
    C   D

_____11. In contrast of his earlier behavior, the young man demon-
              A

strated surprising maturity in the face of severe stress.
         B   C   D

_____12. I told them to take there boots off outside so they would
                          A   B   C

not bring in a lot of snow.
    D

_____13. Try to image what life was like for the early settlers of that
         A   B   C

part of the world.
     D

_____14. Emergency relief, including medicine, clothing, and
                          A

foodstuffs, were sent to the earthquake zone immediately
    B   C

following news of the disaster.
    D

_____15. It was so ferociously not yesterday that our supposed day
                   A   B

of outdoor enjoyment ended with everyone's laying in the
                              C   D

shade.

Check your answers with the error key on page 216.

ERROR KEYS

STYLE—Voice

ERROR KEY

_A_ 1. (*I ate steak* last night.) See rule 3.

_C_ 2.

_C_ 3.

_C_ 4.

_A_ 5. (*The road was built* in two years at a cost of five million dollars.) See rule 1.

_A_ 6. (The people loved their leader and *forgave his mistakes*.) See rule 4.

_A_ 7. (*John answered the phone* on the first ring.) See rule 3.

_C_ 8.

_C_ 9.

_C_ 10.

_C_ 11.

_A_ 12. (As we neared the house, *we could see a small dog* sitting on the porch.) See rule 4.

_A_ 13. (*A lot of crimes were committed* in this neighborhood last month.) See rule 1.

_A_ 14. (If you studied more, *you could easily pass your tests*.) See rules 1 and 4.

_C_ 15.

_C_ 16.

_A_ 17. (*I turned on the light* as I entered my bedroom.) See rules 1 and 4.

_A_ 18. (That electronics company is expanding and *developing many new products*.) See rule 4.

_A_ 19. (*The Battle of Hastings was fought* in 1066.) See rule 2.

_A_ 20. (*Jane put on her earrings* before she went to the party.) See rule 3.

_C_ 21.

_A_ 22. (Claire painted the living room and *laid a new carpet*.) See rule 4.

_A_ 23. (Jack works hard during the week and *spends his free time sailing his new boat*.) See rule 4.

_A_ 24. (*The carefully selected students represented the class well*.) See rule 4.

_A_ 25. (Bob *plays the piano and the guitar*.) See rule 5.

STYLE—Parallelism

ERROR KEY

_X_ 1. (and *to swim*). See rule 1d.

_C_ 2.

_C_ 3.

_X_ 4. (*and the fjords*). See rule 2a.

_C_ 5.

_X_ 6. (*written* a will). See rule 1f.

_C_ 7.

_C_ 8.

_X_ 9. (and *confidence*). See rule 1a.

_C_ 10.

_X_ 11. (or *to study*). See rule 2d.

_X_ 12. (slow *to praise*). See rule 2f.

_C_ 13.

_X_ 14. (and *put* them). See rule 1e.

_X_ 15. (than *playing* golf). See rule 2e.

STYLE—Wordiness

ERROR KEY

_W_ 1. (*The man shook his head*.) OR (*The man said no.*) See rule 3.

_C_ 2.

_C_ 3.

_W_ 4. (Jane went to the store *to buy a new dress*.) See rule 3.

_W_ 5. (*Running through the street*, the thief was apprehended by the police.) See rule 3.

_C_ 6.

_W_ 7. (Bob saw several *expensive* pieces of art.) See rule 2.

_C_ 8.

_W_ 9. (The ballerina *danced for hours*.) See rule 4.

_W_ 10. (Professor Blanton, *the college president*, will speak on this topic.) See rule 2.

_C_ 11.

_C_ 12.

_W_ 13. (*It took us three hours to drive to New York*.) See rule 3.

_C_ 14.

_W_ 15. (*I read the book* in four hours.) See rule 1.

STYLE—Substandard

ERROR KEY

_C_ 1.

_X_ 2. (the reason he was late was *that*). See rule 8.

_C_ 3.

_X_ 4. (*a kind of* car). See rule 4.

_X_ 5. (*"Parallel" means that* objects are). See rule 9.

_C_ 6.

_X_ 7. (*nowhere*). See rule 2.

_C_ 8.

_X_ 9. (*all right*). See rule 3.

_C_ 10.

_X_ 11. (*are not* coming). See rule 1.

_X_ 12. (you do not *suspect*). See rule 7.

_X_ 13. (*A "knock-out" is "a blow that causes unconsciousness."*)
See rule 9.

_C_ 14.

_X_ 15. (*anywhere*). See rule 2.

_X_ 16. (different *from*). See rule 10.

_X_ 17. (*off the* table). See rule 6.

_C_ 18.

_X_ 19. (very *angry with* his professor). See rule 5.

_X_ 20. (*kind of person*). See rule 4.

STYLE—Usage

ERROR KEY

_C_ 1.

_C_ 2.

_C_ 3.

_X_ 4. (surprising *amount* of news). See rule 2.

_X_ 5. (has *risen* enough). See rule 6.

_C_ 6.

_X_ 7. (*between* his children, Betty and John). See rule 1.

_C_ 8.

_X_ 9. (have already *raised*). See rule 6.

_X_ 10. (large *number*). See rule 2.

_C_ 11.

_X_ 12. (dashed quickly *into*). See rule 3.

_X_ 13. (*lying* on the sofa). See rule 5.

_C_ 14.

_X_ 15. (if they *may* have candy). See rule 8.

_C_ 16.

_C_ 17.

_C_ 18.

_X_ 19.   (*taught* him to repair). See rule 7.

_X_ 20.   (had carefully *laid*). See rule 5.

STYLE—Words Often Confused, Group I

ERROR KEY

_X_ 1.   (*already*). See rule 5.

_X_ 2.   (*cloth*). See rule 6.

_C_ 3.

_C_ 4.

_X_ 5.   (*all together*). See rule 4.

_C_ 6.

_X_ 7.   (differed loudly *with*). See rule 8.

_C_ 8.

_X_ 9.   (*beside* the sofa). See rule 2.

_X_ 10.   (*farther*). See rule 10.

_C_ 11.

_X_ 12.   (*emigrate* from). See rule 9.

_X_ 13.   (*advice*). See rule 3.

_X_ 14.   (differs *from*). See rule 8.

_X_ 15.   (*further* instruction). See rule 10.

STYLE—Words Often Confused, Group II

ERROR KEY

_X_ 1.   (*it's* difficult). See rule 5.

_C_ 2.

_X_ 3.   (*principal* fact) OR (The *principle* I would like). See rule 10.

_C_ 4.

_C_ 5.

_X_ 6. (relatively *healthy*). See rule 2.

_X_ 7. (create the *illusion*). See rule 3.

_C_ 8.

_X_ 9. (would not *lose* them). See rule 7.

_C_ 10.

_X_ 11. (*let* him find out). See rule 6.

_C_ 12.

_X_ 13. (*almost* fell off my seat laughing). See rule 8.

_C_ 14.

_X_ 15. (trying to *imply*). See rule 4.

STYLE—Words Often Confused, Group III

ERROR KEY

_X_ 1. (The *weather* is). See rule 6.

_C_ 2.

_C_ 3.

_X_ 4. (*who's* coming). See rule 7.

_X_ 5. (*stationery* stores). See rule 3.

_C_ 6.

_X_ 7. (*their* books). See rule 4.

_X_ 8. (applauded *respectfully*). See rule 1.

_X_ 9. (*to* people). See rule 5.

_C_ 10.

STYLE—Correlative Conjunctions

ERROR KEY

_X_ 1. (neither write *nor* speak)

_C_ 2.

___X___ 3. (both living abroad *and* living).

___X___ 4. (not only the 100-yard dash, *but also* the broad jump)

___C___ 5.

___C___ 6.

___C___ 7.

___C___ 8.

___X___ 9. (*was long*, boring, *and* depressing) OR (long *and* boring, *as well as* depressing). See note a.

___X___ 10. (both deceptive *and* irresponsible)

STYLE—Subject/Verb Agreement

ERROR KEY

___C___ 1.

___X___ 2. (*were* several small boats). See rule 3.

___C___ 3.

___X___ 4. (never *ceases*). See rule 1.

___C___ 5.

___C___ 6.

___X___ 7. (or her children *are* going). See rule 5.

___X___ 8. (the women who *are* responsible). See rule 7.

___X___ 9. (*is* going). See rule 4.

___C___ 10.

STYLE—Parts of Speech

ERROR KEY

___X___ 1. (Bob hopes to *beautify*). See rule 4.

___X___ 2. (a very *happy* man). See rule 2.

___C___ 3.

___X___ 4. (the *reality* of that situation). See rule 1.

_C_ 5.

_C_ 6.

_X_ 7. (his *accuracy*). See rule 1.

_X_ 8. (so *childishly*). See rule 3.

_C_ 9.

_X_ 10. (the *population*). See rule 1.

STYLE—Prepositions (General Use)

ERROR KEY

_C_ 1.

_X_ 2. (*by* car). See rule 5.

_C_ 3.

_C_ 4.

_X_ 5. (walks *like* his father). See rule 10.

_X_ 6. (*with* a key). See rule 5.

_C_ 7.

_X_ 8. (*by* the yard) See rule 9.

_C_ 9.

_X_ 10. (*for* a newspaper). See rule 7.

_C_ 11.

_X_ 12. (leg *of* the chair). See rule 8.

_X_ 13. (pounds *of* butter). See rule 9.

_C_ 14.

_X_ 15. (*at* 7:00). See rule 3.

STYLE—Prepositions in Combinations

ERROR KEY

_X_ 1. (agree *with* your father). See rule 1.

_X_ 2. (arrived *in*). See rule 1.

_C_ 3.

_X_ 4. (depends *on* your schedule). See rule 1.

_C_ 5.

_X_ 6. (surprised *at*) OR (surprised *by*). See rule 3.

_C_ 7.

_X_ 8. (famous *for* its beautiful mountains). See rule 3.

_C_ 9.

_X_ 10. (compare favorably *to*) OR (compare favorably *with*). See rule 2.

_C_ 11.

_X_ 12. (tired *of* waiting). See rule 3.

_X_ 13. (comment *on*). See rule 1.

_X_ 14. (familiar *with*). See rule 3.

_X_ 15. (in search *of*). See rule 4.

CHAPTER QUIZ—Style

ERROR KEY

Some of the incorrect answers contain more than one kind of error. However, in general, we have limited our references to errors to those points contained in *Style*.

_C_ 1. (A) See *Parallelism*, page 159.
(B) Same as A
(C) Correct
(D) Same as A

_C_ 2. (A) See *Substandard*, page 166.
(B) Same as A
(C) Correct
(D) Same as A

_D_ 3. (A) See *Correlative Conjunctions*, page 187.
(B) Same as A
(C) Same as A
(D) Correct

__B__ 4. (A) See *Prepositions in Combinations*, page 198.
      (B) Correct
      (C) Same as A
      (D) Same as A

__B__ 5. (A) See *Words Often Confused*, Group III, page 184.
      (B) Correct
      (C) Same as A
      (D) Incomplete verb form

__C__ 6. (A) See *Substandard*, page 166.
      (B) Same as A
      (C) Correct
      (D) Same as A and *Voice*, page 156.

__C__ 7. (A) See *Usage*, page 169.
      (B) Same as A
      (C) Correct
      (D) Same as A

__A__ 8. (A) Correct
      (B) See *Parallelism*, page 159.
      (C) Same as B
      (D) The meaning of *loveliness* does not fit here.

__B__ 9. (A) See *Voice*, page 156.
      (B) Correct
      (C) See *Verbs—Verbals*, page 87.
      (D) Same as A

__A__ 10. (A) Correct
      (B) See *Prepositions in Combinations*, page 198.
      (C) Same as B
      (D) Same as B

__B__ 11. (A) See *Wordiness*, page 162.
      (B) Correct
      (C) Same as A
      (D) See *Voice*, page 156.

__A__ 12. (A) Correct
      (B) See *Wordiness,* page 162.
      (C) Same as B
      (D) Same as B

__C__ 13. (A) See *Parts of Speech*, page 193.
      (B) Same as A
      (C) Correct
      (D) Same as A

__B__ 14. (A) See *Correlative Conjunctions*, page 187.
      (B) Correct
      (C) Same as A
      (D) Same as A

__B__ 15.   (A) See *Parts of Speech*, page 193.
            (B) Correct
            (C) Same as A
            (D) Same as A

__C__ 1.   (*and*). See *Correlative Conjunctions*, page 187.

__D__ 2.   (*plain*-looking). See *Words Often Confused*, Group II, page 179.

__B__ 3.   (*as*). See *Prepositions (General Use)*, page 195.

__D__ 4.   (had been *raised*). See *Usage*, page 169.

__B__ 5.   (*bought supplies*). See *Voice*, page 156.

__B__ 6.   (*Sahara Desert*). See *Words Often Confused*, Group I, page 174.

__C__ 7.   (in favor *of*). See *Prepositions in Combinations*, page 198.

__D__ 8.   (*working*). See *Parallelism*, page 159.

__C__ 9.   (consisted *of*). See *Prepositions in Combinations*, page 198.

__A__ 10.   (*is*). See *Subject/Verb Agreement*, page 189.

__A__ 11.   (contrast *to*). See *Prepositions in Combinations*, page 198.

__A__ 12.   (*their*). See *Words Often Confused*, Group III, page 184.

__A__ 13.   (to *imagine*). See *Parts of Speech*, page 193.

__C__ 14.   (*was* sent). See *Subject/Verb Agreement*, page 189.

__D__ 15.   (*lying*). See *Usage*, page 169.

ANSWER SHEETS FOR PRACTICE TEST A

1 Ⓐ Ⓑ Ⓒ Ⓓ   11 Ⓐ Ⓑ Ⓒ Ⓓ   21 Ⓐ Ⓑ Ⓒ Ⓓ   31 Ⓐ Ⓑ Ⓒ Ⓓ

2 Ⓐ Ⓑ Ⓒ Ⓓ   12 Ⓐ Ⓑ Ⓒ Ⓓ   22 Ⓐ Ⓑ Ⓒ Ⓓ   32 Ⓐ Ⓑ Ⓒ Ⓓ

3 Ⓐ Ⓑ Ⓒ Ⓓ   13 Ⓐ Ⓑ Ⓒ Ⓓ   23 Ⓐ Ⓑ Ⓒ Ⓓ   33 Ⓐ Ⓑ Ⓒ Ⓓ

4 Ⓐ Ⓑ Ⓒ Ⓓ   14 Ⓐ Ⓑ Ⓒ Ⓓ   24 Ⓐ Ⓑ Ⓒ Ⓓ   34 Ⓐ Ⓑ Ⓒ Ⓓ

5 Ⓐ Ⓑ Ⓒ Ⓓ   15 Ⓐ Ⓑ Ⓒ Ⓓ   25 Ⓐ Ⓑ Ⓒ Ⓓ   35 Ⓐ Ⓑ Ⓒ Ⓓ

6 Ⓐ Ⓑ Ⓒ Ⓓ   16 Ⓐ Ⓑ Ⓒ Ⓓ   26 Ⓐ Ⓑ Ⓒ Ⓓ   36 Ⓐ Ⓑ Ⓒ Ⓓ

7 Ⓐ Ⓑ Ⓒ Ⓓ   17 Ⓐ Ⓑ Ⓒ Ⓓ   27 Ⓐ Ⓑ Ⓒ Ⓓ   37 Ⓐ Ⓑ Ⓒ Ⓓ

8 Ⓐ Ⓑ Ⓒ Ⓓ   18 Ⓐ Ⓑ Ⓒ Ⓓ   28 Ⓐ Ⓑ Ⓒ Ⓓ   38 Ⓐ Ⓑ Ⓒ Ⓓ

9 Ⓐ Ⓑ Ⓒ Ⓓ   19 Ⓐ Ⓑ Ⓒ Ⓓ   29 Ⓐ Ⓑ Ⓒ Ⓓ   39 Ⓐ Ⓑ Ⓒ Ⓓ

10 Ⓐ Ⓑ Ⓒ Ⓓ   20 Ⓐ Ⓑ Ⓒ Ⓓ   30 Ⓐ Ⓑ Ⓒ Ⓓ   40 Ⓐ Ⓑ Ⓒ Ⓓ

1 Ⓐ Ⓑ Ⓒ Ⓓ   11 Ⓐ Ⓑ Ⓒ Ⓓ   21 Ⓐ Ⓑ Ⓒ Ⓓ   31 Ⓐ Ⓑ Ⓒ Ⓓ

2 Ⓐ Ⓑ Ⓒ Ⓓ   12 Ⓐ Ⓑ Ⓒ Ⓓ   22 Ⓐ Ⓑ Ⓒ Ⓓ   32 Ⓐ Ⓑ Ⓒ Ⓓ

3 Ⓐ Ⓑ Ⓒ Ⓓ   13 Ⓐ Ⓑ Ⓒ Ⓓ   23 Ⓐ Ⓑ Ⓒ Ⓓ   33 Ⓐ Ⓑ Ⓒ Ⓓ

4 Ⓐ Ⓑ Ⓒ Ⓓ   14 Ⓐ Ⓑ Ⓒ Ⓓ   24 Ⓐ Ⓑ Ⓒ Ⓓ   34 Ⓐ Ⓑ Ⓒ Ⓓ

5 Ⓐ Ⓑ Ⓒ Ⓓ   15 Ⓐ Ⓑ Ⓒ Ⓓ   25 Ⓐ Ⓑ Ⓒ Ⓓ   35 Ⓐ Ⓑ Ⓒ Ⓓ

6 Ⓐ Ⓑ Ⓒ Ⓓ   16 Ⓐ Ⓑ Ⓒ Ⓓ   26 Ⓐ Ⓑ Ⓒ Ⓓ   36 Ⓐ Ⓑ Ⓒ Ⓓ

7 Ⓐ Ⓑ Ⓒ Ⓓ   17 Ⓐ Ⓑ Ⓒ Ⓓ   27 Ⓐ Ⓑ Ⓒ Ⓓ   37 Ⓐ Ⓑ Ⓒ Ⓓ

8 Ⓐ Ⓑ Ⓒ Ⓓ   18 Ⓐ Ⓑ Ⓒ Ⓓ   28 Ⓐ Ⓑ Ⓒ Ⓓ   38 Ⓐ Ⓑ Ⓒ Ⓓ

9 Ⓐ Ⓑ Ⓒ Ⓓ   19 Ⓐ Ⓑ Ⓒ Ⓓ   29 Ⓐ Ⓑ Ⓒ Ⓓ   39 Ⓐ Ⓑ Ⓒ Ⓓ

10 Ⓐ Ⓑ Ⓒ Ⓓ   20 Ⓐ Ⓑ Ⓒ Ⓓ   30 Ⓐ Ⓑ Ⓒ Ⓓ   40 Ⓐ Ⓑ Ⓒ Ⓓ

ANSWER SHEETS FOR
PRACTICE TEST B

1 Ⓐ Ⓑ Ⓒ Ⓓ	11 Ⓐ Ⓑ Ⓒ Ⓓ	21 Ⓐ Ⓑ Ⓒ Ⓓ	31 Ⓐ Ⓑ Ⓒ Ⓓ
2 Ⓐ Ⓑ Ⓒ Ⓓ	12 Ⓐ Ⓑ Ⓒ Ⓓ	22 Ⓐ Ⓑ Ⓒ Ⓓ	32 Ⓐ Ⓑ Ⓒ Ⓓ
3 Ⓐ Ⓑ Ⓒ Ⓓ	13 Ⓐ Ⓑ Ⓒ Ⓓ	23 Ⓐ Ⓑ Ⓒ Ⓓ	33 Ⓐ Ⓑ Ⓒ Ⓓ
4 Ⓐ Ⓑ Ⓒ Ⓓ	14 Ⓐ Ⓑ Ⓒ Ⓓ	24 Ⓐ Ⓑ Ⓒ Ⓓ	34 Ⓐ Ⓑ Ⓒ Ⓓ
5 Ⓐ Ⓑ Ⓒ Ⓓ	15 Ⓐ Ⓑ Ⓒ Ⓓ	25 Ⓐ Ⓑ Ⓒ Ⓓ	35 Ⓐ Ⓑ Ⓒ Ⓓ
6 Ⓐ Ⓑ Ⓒ Ⓓ	16 Ⓐ Ⓑ Ⓒ Ⓓ	26 Ⓐ Ⓑ Ⓒ Ⓓ	36 Ⓐ Ⓑ Ⓒ Ⓓ
7 Ⓐ Ⓑ Ⓒ Ⓓ	17 Ⓐ Ⓑ Ⓒ Ⓓ	27 Ⓐ Ⓑ Ⓒ Ⓓ	37 Ⓐ Ⓑ Ⓒ Ⓓ
8 Ⓐ Ⓑ Ⓒ Ⓓ	18 Ⓐ Ⓑ Ⓒ Ⓓ	28 Ⓐ Ⓑ Ⓒ Ⓓ	38 Ⓐ Ⓑ Ⓒ Ⓓ
9 Ⓐ Ⓑ Ⓒ Ⓓ	19 Ⓐ Ⓑ Ⓒ Ⓓ	29 Ⓐ Ⓑ Ⓒ Ⓓ	39 Ⓐ Ⓑ Ⓒ Ⓓ
10 Ⓐ Ⓑ Ⓒ Ⓓ	20 Ⓐ Ⓑ Ⓒ Ⓓ	30 Ⓐ Ⓑ Ⓒ Ⓓ	40 Ⓐ Ⓑ Ⓒ Ⓓ

1 Ⓐ Ⓑ Ⓒ Ⓓ	11 Ⓐ Ⓑ Ⓒ Ⓓ	21 Ⓐ Ⓑ Ⓒ Ⓓ	31 Ⓐ Ⓑ Ⓒ Ⓓ
2 Ⓐ Ⓑ Ⓒ Ⓓ	12 Ⓐ Ⓑ Ⓒ Ⓓ	22 Ⓐ Ⓑ Ⓒ Ⓓ	32 Ⓐ Ⓑ Ⓒ Ⓓ
3 Ⓐ Ⓑ Ⓒ Ⓓ	13 Ⓐ Ⓑ Ⓒ Ⓓ	23 Ⓐ Ⓑ Ⓒ Ⓓ	33 Ⓐ Ⓑ Ⓒ Ⓓ
4 Ⓐ Ⓑ Ⓒ Ⓓ	14 Ⓐ Ⓑ Ⓒ Ⓓ	24 Ⓐ Ⓑ Ⓒ Ⓓ	34 Ⓐ Ⓑ Ⓒ Ⓓ
5 Ⓐ Ⓑ Ⓒ Ⓓ	15 Ⓐ Ⓑ Ⓒ Ⓓ	25 Ⓐ Ⓑ Ⓒ Ⓓ	35 Ⓐ Ⓑ Ⓒ Ⓓ
6 Ⓐ Ⓑ Ⓒ Ⓓ	16 Ⓐ Ⓑ Ⓒ Ⓓ	26 Ⓐ Ⓑ Ⓒ Ⓓ	36 Ⓐ Ⓑ Ⓒ Ⓓ
7 Ⓐ Ⓑ Ⓒ Ⓓ	17 Ⓐ Ⓑ Ⓒ Ⓓ	27 Ⓐ Ⓑ Ⓒ Ⓓ	37 Ⓐ Ⓑ Ⓒ Ⓓ
8 Ⓐ Ⓑ Ⓒ Ⓓ	18 Ⓐ Ⓑ Ⓒ Ⓓ	28 Ⓐ Ⓑ Ⓒ Ⓓ	38 Ⓐ Ⓑ Ⓒ Ⓓ
9 Ⓐ Ⓑ Ⓒ Ⓓ	19 Ⓐ Ⓑ Ⓒ Ⓓ	29 Ⓐ Ⓑ Ⓒ Ⓓ	39 Ⓐ Ⓑ Ⓒ Ⓓ
10 Ⓐ Ⓑ Ⓒ Ⓓ	20 Ⓐ Ⓑ Ⓒ Ⓓ	30 Ⓐ Ⓑ Ⓒ Ⓓ	40 Ⓐ Ⓑ Ⓒ Ⓓ

ANSWER SHEETS FOR
PRACTICE TEST C

1 Ⓐ Ⓑ Ⓒ Ⓓ   11 Ⓐ Ⓑ Ⓒ Ⓓ   21 Ⓐ Ⓑ Ⓒ Ⓓ   31 Ⓐ Ⓑ Ⓒ Ⓓ
2 Ⓐ Ⓑ Ⓒ Ⓓ   12 Ⓐ Ⓑ Ⓒ Ⓓ   22 Ⓐ Ⓑ Ⓒ Ⓓ   32 Ⓐ Ⓑ Ⓒ Ⓓ
3 Ⓐ Ⓑ Ⓒ Ⓓ   13 Ⓐ Ⓑ Ⓒ Ⓓ   23 Ⓐ Ⓑ Ⓒ Ⓓ   33 Ⓐ Ⓑ Ⓒ Ⓓ
4 Ⓐ Ⓑ Ⓒ Ⓓ   14 Ⓐ Ⓑ Ⓒ Ⓓ   24 Ⓐ Ⓑ Ⓒ Ⓓ   34 Ⓐ Ⓑ Ⓒ Ⓓ
5 Ⓐ Ⓑ Ⓒ Ⓓ   15 Ⓐ Ⓑ Ⓒ Ⓓ   25 Ⓐ Ⓑ Ⓒ Ⓓ   35 Ⓐ Ⓑ Ⓒ Ⓓ
6 Ⓐ Ⓑ Ⓒ Ⓓ   16 Ⓐ Ⓑ Ⓒ Ⓓ   26 Ⓐ Ⓑ Ⓒ Ⓓ   36 Ⓐ Ⓑ Ⓒ Ⓓ
7 Ⓐ Ⓑ Ⓒ Ⓓ   17 Ⓐ Ⓑ Ⓒ Ⓓ   27 Ⓐ Ⓑ Ⓒ Ⓓ   37 Ⓐ Ⓑ Ⓒ Ⓓ
8 Ⓐ Ⓑ Ⓒ Ⓓ   18 Ⓐ Ⓑ Ⓒ Ⓓ   28 Ⓐ Ⓑ Ⓒ Ⓓ   38 Ⓐ Ⓑ Ⓒ Ⓓ
9 Ⓐ Ⓑ Ⓒ Ⓓ   19 Ⓐ Ⓑ Ⓒ Ⓓ   29 Ⓐ Ⓑ Ⓒ Ⓓ   39 Ⓐ Ⓑ Ⓒ Ⓓ
10 Ⓐ Ⓑ Ⓒ Ⓓ   20 Ⓐ Ⓑ Ⓒ Ⓓ   30 Ⓐ Ⓑ Ⓒ Ⓓ   40 Ⓐ Ⓑ Ⓒ Ⓓ

1 Ⓐ Ⓑ Ⓒ Ⓓ   11 Ⓐ Ⓑ Ⓒ Ⓓ   21 Ⓐ Ⓑ Ⓒ Ⓓ   31 Ⓐ Ⓑ Ⓒ Ⓓ
2 Ⓐ Ⓑ Ⓒ Ⓓ   12 Ⓐ Ⓑ Ⓒ Ⓓ   22 Ⓐ Ⓑ Ⓒ Ⓓ   32 Ⓐ Ⓑ Ⓒ Ⓓ
3 Ⓐ Ⓑ Ⓒ Ⓓ   13 Ⓐ Ⓑ Ⓒ Ⓓ   23 Ⓐ Ⓑ Ⓒ Ⓓ   33 Ⓐ Ⓑ Ⓒ Ⓓ
4 Ⓐ Ⓑ Ⓒ Ⓓ   14 Ⓐ Ⓑ Ⓒ Ⓓ   24 Ⓐ Ⓑ Ⓒ Ⓓ   34 Ⓐ Ⓑ Ⓒ Ⓓ
5 Ⓐ Ⓑ Ⓒ Ⓓ   15 Ⓐ Ⓑ Ⓒ Ⓓ   25 Ⓐ Ⓑ Ⓒ Ⓓ   35 Ⓐ Ⓑ Ⓒ Ⓓ
6 Ⓐ Ⓑ Ⓒ Ⓓ   16 Ⓐ Ⓑ Ⓒ Ⓓ   26 Ⓐ Ⓑ Ⓒ Ⓓ   36 Ⓐ Ⓑ Ⓒ Ⓓ
7 Ⓐ Ⓑ Ⓒ Ⓓ   17 Ⓐ Ⓑ Ⓒ Ⓓ   27 Ⓐ Ⓑ Ⓒ Ⓓ   37 Ⓐ Ⓑ Ⓒ Ⓓ
8 Ⓐ Ⓑ Ⓒ Ⓓ   18 Ⓐ Ⓑ Ⓒ Ⓓ   28 Ⓐ Ⓑ Ⓒ Ⓓ   38 Ⓐ Ⓑ Ⓒ Ⓓ
9 Ⓐ Ⓑ Ⓒ Ⓓ   19 Ⓐ Ⓑ Ⓒ Ⓓ   29 Ⓐ Ⓑ Ⓒ Ⓓ   39 Ⓐ Ⓑ Ⓒ Ⓓ
10 Ⓐ Ⓑ Ⓒ Ⓓ   20 Ⓐ Ⓑ Ⓒ Ⓓ   30 Ⓐ Ⓑ Ⓒ Ⓓ   40 Ⓐ Ⓑ Ⓒ Ⓓ

ADDITIONAL ANSWER SHEETS

1 (A) (B) (C) (D)   11 (A) (B) (C) (D)   21 (A) (B) (C) (D)   31 (A) (B) (C) (D)

2 (A) (B) (C) (D)   12 (A) (B) (C) (D)   22 (A) (B) (C) (D)   32 (A) (B) (C) (D)

3 (A) (B) (C) (D)   13 (A) (B) (C) (D)   23 (A) (B) (C) (D)   33 (A) (B) (C) (D)

4 (A) (B) (C) (D)   14 (A) (B) (C) (D)   24 (A) (B) (C) (D)   34 (A) (B) (C) (D)

5 (A) (B) (C) (D)   15 (A) (B) (C) (D)   25 (A) (B) (C) (D)   35 (A) (B) (C) (D)

6 (A) (B) (C) (D)   16 (A) (B) (C) (D)   26 (A) (B) (C) (D)   36 (A) (B) (C) (D)

7 (A) (B) (C) (D)   17 (A) (B) (C) (D)   27 (A) (B) (C) (D)   37 (A) (B) (C) (D)

8 (A) (B) (C) (D)   18 (A) (B) (C) (D)   28 (A) (B) (C) (D)   38 (A) (B) (C) (D)

9 (A) (B) (C) (D)   19 (A) (B) (C) (D)   29 (A) (B) (C) (D)   39 (A) (B) (C) (D)

10 (A) (B) (C) (D)   20 (A) (B) (C) (D)   30 (A) (B) (C) (D)   40 (A) (B) (C) (D)

1 (A) (B) (C) (D)   11 (A) (B) (C) (D)   21 (A) (B) (C) (D)   31 (A) (B) (C) (D)

2 (A) (B) (C) (D)   12 (A) (B) (C) (D)   22 (A) (B) (C) (D)   32 (A) (B) (C) (D)

3 (A) (B) (C) (D)   13 (A) (B) (C) (D)   23 (A) (B) (C) (D)   33 (A) (B) (C) (D)

4 (A) (B) (C) (D)   14 (A) (B) (C) (D)   24 (A) (B) (C) (D)   34 (A) (B) (C) (D)

5 (A) (B) (C) (D)   15 (A) (B) (C) (D)   25 (A) (B) (C) (D)   35 (A) (B) (C) (D)

6 (A) (B) (C) (D)   16 (A) (B) (C) (D)   26 (A) (B) (C) (D)   36 (A) (B) (C) (D)

7 (A) (B) (C) (D)   17 (A) (B) (C) (D)   27 (A) (B) (C) (D)   37 (A) (B) (C) (D)

8 (A) (B) (C) (D)   18 (A) (B) (C) (D)   28 (A) (B) (C) (D)   38 (A) (B) (C) (D)

9 (A) (B) (C) (D)   19 (A) (B) (C) (D)   29 (A) (B) (C) (D)   39 (A) (B) (C) (D)

10 (A) (B) (C) (D)   20 (A) (B) (C) (D)   30 (A) (B) (C) (D)   40 (A) (B) (C) (D)

XIII

INTRODUCTION TO PRACTICE TESTS

The following three tests simulate the Structure and Written Expression section of the TOEFL. In order for you to take these practice tests under conditions most nearly like those of the real TOEFL, use the answer sheets that are provided on the previous pages. Each test is designed to be completed in 25 minutes (37 to 38 seconds per question). Make sure to set a timer or ask a friend to time you. After completing these tests, check your answers with the error keys that follow, which will refer you to the specific grammatical points you need to review. There are extra answer sheets provided so that you may re-take the tests.

Practice Test A

Time: 25 minutes

DIRECTIONS: Choose the best answer (A, B, C, or D) to complete each of the following sentences. Blacken the space on your answer sheet that corresponds to the best choice.

1. It was _____ that we went for a hike in the mountains.

   (A) so nice a day
   (B) such nice day
   (C) so nice day
   (D) such nice a day

2. I was surprised to see _____ at the concert.

   (A) those number of people
   (B) that amount of people
   (C) that number of people
   (D) those amount of people

3. The art museum is internationally acclaimed not only for its sixteenth-century Flemish collection _____ for its early Picasso collection.

    (A) and
    (B) but
    (C) but also
    (D) as well as

4. _____ that the hope for cancer control may lie in the use of a vaccine.

    (A) To believe
    (B) It is believed
    (C) Believing
    (D) The belief

5. Everyone was _____ the threat of military intervention in that area.

    (A) frightened for
    (B) frightened
    (C) frightened to
    (D) frightened by

6. If Dorothy had not been badly hurt in a car accident, _____ in last month's marathon.

    (A) she would participate
    (B) she participated
    (C) she would have participated
    (D) she would had participate

7. On our last trip to Europe, we spent a lot of time visiting _____ churches and castles.

    (A) old enough
    (B) very old
    (C) enough old
    (D) too old

8. Our success depends _____ the project by December.

    (A) on finishing
    (B) finishing
    (C) about finishing
    (D) on to finish

9. Be sure to wake _____ at 7:00 A.M.

   (A) we
   (B) Paul and me
   (C) us, Paul and I
   (D) Paul and I

10. When Betty met Sue, _____.

   (A) she was a student at Stanford.
   (B) Sue was a student at Stanford.
   (C) she is a student at Stanford.
   (D) at Stanford Sue was a student.

11. Nancy sometimes wishes that she _____ in a small town.

   (A) was not living
   (B) did not lived
   (C) does not live
   (D) were not living

12. When the professor called on him, _____.

   (A) John repeated again the correct answer
   (B) John repeated the correct answer
   (C) John repeated the answer which was correct
   (D) the correct answer was repeated by John

13. These seats are reserved for _____.

   (A) those on the executive committee
   (B) they on the executive committee
   (C) them on the executive committee
   (D) those who find themselves in the position of being on the executive committee

14. Barbara has been pursuing a career in architecture _____ she graduated in May.

   (A) when
   (B) until
   (C) for
   (D) since

15. Our buyer has gone to New York _____ the new fall clothes.

   (A) to choose
   (B) for to choose
   (C) for choosing
   (D) for having chosen

DIRECTIONS: Blacken the space corresponding
to the letter of the *incorrect* part of the sentence
(or the one that should be rewritten) on your
answer sheet.

16. <u>Since</u> William had been seriously ill <u>for</u> several months, his
    A   B

    parents were concerned <u>about</u> <u>him wanting</u> to return to school
                           C   D

    full-time.

17. The mother cried <u>as</u> her child <u>laid</u> <u>on</u> the examination table
                      A   B   C

    <u>after</u> the accident.
    D

18. The students were quite surprised <u>to find</u> <u>these kind</u> of archeo-
                                       A   B

    logical ruins in the particular area <u>that</u> <u>they</u> had chosen for the dig.
                                         C   D

19. John stayed <u>up</u> all night <u>long</u> <u>trying</u> to solve a <u>physic</u> problem.
                A   B   C   D

20. Michael wants <u>to become</u> a general practitioner <u>as</u> his father
                  A   B

    and to move to a small town <u>as soon as</u> he <u>graduates</u>.
                                C   D

21. In spite of their <u>trepidations</u>, the parents let their two <u>oldest</u>
                      A   B

    children <u>driven</u> alone to New Mexico <u>to ski</u>.
             C   D

22. Life in modern society <u>lacks</u> the sense of <u>permanent</u> that is <u>so</u>
                           A   B   C

    important to social <u>stability</u>.
                        D

23. <u>As soon as</u> they <u>will finish</u> the new business <u>administration</u>
    A   B   C

    building, our offices are going <u>to be</u> moved.
                                    D

24. In spite of suffering some minor inconveniences, Dr. Blake and
       A   B

    his wife enjoyed living in a three-hundred-years-old house in
              C   D

    London last summer.

25. If Tom would have sent in his papers sooner, he would have been
         A   B   C

    accepted for this semester.
      D

26. Professor Layton was equally fond of his two children, but he
              A   B

    had to admit that he found the youngest an easier child
                       C

    to handle.
     D

27. By the beginning of next year, much of the people who live in
     A   B   C

    that area may have difficulty finding employment.
                    D

28. Even though the child pretended sleeping, when we opened the
      A   B   C

    bedroom door we were not deceived.
                   D

29. Be careful to give the caterers a accurate count of the number
          A   B

    of people whom you expect to go to the wedding reception.
         C   D

30. Ever since he arrived, he has been complaining about constantly
      A   B   C   D

    the weather.

31. The living room was enough large to accommodate two long
       A   B   C

    sofas easily.
      D

32. Approving of my choice of colleges, my father said that he was
    A

    willing to completely pay for all the costs of my education.
      B   C   D

33. In spite of the exceedingly favorable financial benefits she is re-
    A   B

    ceiving, Linda now wishes that she was not stationed in Alaska
                                        C

    for three years.
    D

34. When the seamstress tried to sew the button on with a plastic
             A   B   C

    needle, it broke.
           D

35. We all laughed when Helen said she could not remember what
          A   B   C

    day was it.
        D

36. The children soon forgot that it was them, their parents, who
                                  A   B   C

    had encouraged them to continue their education.
                          D

37. Having ran for three miles, I was exhausted but exhilarated.
    A   B   C   D

38. Harold announced that he could not longer tolerate the condi-
                       A   B

    tions of the contract under which he was working.
          C   D

39. Our company looks forward to have you on staff, and we will as-
                                A   B   C

    sist you in any way possible in order to make your move pleasant.
                       D

40. The theater arranged a private <u>showing</u> of the film for Peter and
                                        A

<u>I</u> <u>so that</u> we could review <u>it</u> before our deadline.
B   C   D

Check your answers with the error key on page 240.

Practice Test B

Time—25 minutes

DIRECTIONS: Choose the best answer (A, B, C, or D) to complete each of the following sentences. Blacken the space on your answer sheet that corresponds to the best choice.

1. There _____ in that part of the country.

   (A) are not much industry
   (B) is not many industry
   (C) are not many industry
   (D) is not much industry

2. The *Marcus Aurelius*, _____ went down at sea in 1970, is reputed to have had great wealth on board.

   (A) that which
   (B) which
   (C) who
   (D) what

3. _____ since he lost his job.

   (A) He has been feeling bad
   (B) He is feeling badly
   (C) He had been feeling badly
   (D) He is feeling bad

4. Let's put a new _____ on the window sill.

   (A) flower's box
   (B) flowers' box
   (C) flower box
   (D) flowers box

5. I let my cousin _____ my car when he came to visit me.

   (A) to borrow
   (B) borrow
   (C) borrowing
   (D) borrowed

6. John remembered his parents' anniversary and_____.

   (A) sent them some flowers
   (B) to them sent some flowers
   (C) sent to them some flowers
   (D) some flowers to them sent

7. The plans for that building were drawn up in 1965, but _____.

   (A) their implementation was not put into action until 1970
   (B) the plans for that building were not implemented until 1970
   (C) were not implemented and started until 1970
   (D) were not implemented until 1970

8. The doctor _____.

   (A) adviced that Jim lie down every afternoon
   (B) adviced that Jim lay down every afternoon
   (C) advised that Jim lie down every afternoon
   (D) advised that Jim lay down every afternoon

9. John will most likely _____, but Kathy will probably stay home.

   (A) coming
   (B) be come
   (C) come
   (D) had come

10. _____ told us to turn our topics in by Friday.

    (A) Our professor he
    (B) Our professor who
    (C) Our professor
    (D) Our professor that

11. During her vacation in Europe, Margaret visited museums, went shopping, and _____ a lot of interesting people.

    (A) had met
    (B) was meeting
    (C) met
    (D) has been meeting

12. It was essential that we _____ the lease before the end of the month.

   (A) sign
   (B) signed
   (C) had signed
   (D) were signing

13. The opening of the new freeway has made traffic conditions in the city _____.

   (A) more good
   (B) the better
   (C) better
   (D) more better

14. If their train arrives _____ not make it to the theater on time.

   (A) lately, we will
   (B) late, we would
   (C) more later, we will
   (D) late, we will

15. When traveling in a foreign country, one should be careful to carry _____ at all times.

   (A) their passport
   (B) your passport
   (C) one's passport
   (D) hers passport

DIRECTIONS: Blacken the space corresponding to the *incorrect* part of the sentence (or the one that should be rewritten) on your answer sheet.

16. Lawrence never lost the respect for his parents who had strug-
                        A   B
   gled so hard to put him through medical school.
                    C   D

17. I doubt weather he will enter the doctoral program this fall
              A   B
   because of his financial problems.
       C   D

18. If Jackie and Mary <u>had been</u> <u>in</u> <u>better</u> physical condition, they
                        A   B   C

    <u>might enjoyed</u> the hike more.
         D

19. <u>Not having passed</u> the law exam, <u>the</u> state refused <u>to issue him</u>
          A   B   C

    a license <u>to practice.</u>
                   D

20. The <u>interesting</u> designed stairway led <u>directly</u> to a large ball-
              A   B

    room <u>where</u> everyone <u>was waiting</u> for us.
            C   D

21. <u>Even though</u> they <u>have been looking</u> for an apartment <u>for</u> a month
          A   B   C

    now, they have not been able to find one <u>anywheres.</u>
                                                  D

22. I <u>have reserved</u> six <u>front-row</u> seats <u>for</u> the basketball <u>play-off</u>
          A   B   C   D

    game last night.

23. The five hours of classes the students have every day are

    <u>audio-lingual</u>, reading, writing, <u>laboratory</u>, and <u>to choose</u>
          A   B   C

    an extra <u>special-interest</u> course.
                    D

24. The crops are already <u>showing</u> signs of <u>dehydration</u> and prob-
                              A   B

    ably cannot survive <u>another</u> week without <u>no</u> rain.
                            C   D

25. The children had <u>such difficult time</u> when they <u>began</u> school in
                          A   B

    their new neighborhood that their parents decided <u>never</u> <u>to move</u>
                                                          C   D

    again.

26. He <u>had</u> his tailor <u>made</u> an exotic <u>oriental-looking</u> robe for
           A   B   C

    <u>opening</u> night.
        D

27. Teamwork <u>requires</u> that a player <u>pass</u> the ball to <u>whomever</u> is in
              A   B   C

the <u>best</u> position to make the goal.
    D

28. There were never any secrets <u>among</u> my sister and <u>me</u> <u>when</u> we
                            A   B C

<u>were growing up.</u>
    D

29. Dr. Lacey was the kind of administrator <u>which</u> tried <u>to maintain</u>
                                        A   B

high morale <u>among</u> his staff by <u>encouraging</u> open
               C   D

communication.

30. Let's take one of <u>this</u> pamphlets and <u>look up</u> the special flights
                   A   B

to Hawaii <u>in</u> November.
<u> C </u>   D

31. Samuel's new position <u>as</u> head of the editorial staff is <u>certainly</u> a
                     A   B

more demanding <u>one</u> than <u>Henry.</u>
             C   D

32. Susan was determined <u>to leave</u> the office <u>by</u> 4:30 <u>for catching</u>
                       A   B   C

the early train <u>home.</u>
            D

33. The newlyweds found a style of living <u>in Italy</u> <u>as</u> <u>satisfying</u> that
                                 A   B   C

they wished that they <u>could stay</u> there forever.
                   D

34. <u>Those</u> who <u>had already purchased</u> tickets were instructed to go
    A   B

to gate <u>first</u> <u>immediately.</u>
       C   D

35. The cost <u>of</u> gasoline <u>has raised</u> <u>tremendously</u> in the last
         A   B   C

<u>eight-month</u> period.
    D

36. <u>It</u> is important that you <u>turned off</u> the heater every morning
     A   B

     <u>before</u> you <u>leave</u> for class.
        C   D

37. With regard <u>to</u> your letter of October 26, we are <u>quiet</u> disap-
                    A   B

     pointed <u>to learn</u> that you are <u>unable</u> to accept the job at this time.
                 C   D

38. Dr. Alvarez looked <u>tiredly</u> <u>as</u> he approached the podium <u>to give</u>
                        A   B   C

     his farewell speech to the <u>graduating</u> class.
                                    D

39. <u>Their</u> office has <u>not</u> <u>still</u> returned the original document to <u>us</u>.
     A   B   C   D

40. I was <u>very</u> embarrassed at the <u>inauguration</u> last week when I <u>set</u>
           A   B   C

     in the wrong chair on the <u>stage</u>.
                                  D

Check your answers with the error key on page 242.

Practice Test C

Time: 25 minutes

DIRECTIONS: Choose the best answer (A, B, C,
or D) to complete each of the following sentences.
Blacken the corresponding space for the best
choice on your answer sheet.

1. One should be careful to check the grease and oil in _____
    _____ periodically.

    (A) their car
    (B) one's car
    (C) our car
    (D) your car

2. I wish I had not signed that contract without _____.

   (A) first having consulted a lawyer
   (B) not first having consulted a lawyer
   (C) first having consulted lawyer
   (D) first having consulting a lawyer

3. He likes _____ classical music on the piano.

   (A) only to play
   (B) to only play
   (C) only playing
   (D) to play only

4. The reason they are not coming is _____.

   (A) because they are angry with the hosts
   (B) that they are mad at the hosts
   (C) that they are angry with the hosts
   (D) because they are mad at the hosts

5. I went to my adviser to ask him _____.

   (A) what courses should I take
   (B) should I take what courses
   (C) I should take what courses
   (D) what courses I should take

6. He _____ before spring break.

   (A) hopes to completely finish his term paper
   (B) hopes to finish his term paper completely
   (C) hopes completely to finish his term paper
   (D) hopes to finish completely his term paper

7. Learning to do routine car maintenance oneself is often easier _____ competent people to do it.

   (A) as finding
   (B) than to find
   (C) than finding
   (D) as to find

8. Of all the sports he played, _____.

   (A) he liked tennis least
   (B) it was tennis which was his least liked
   (C) tennis was liked least by him
   (D) tennis was disliked by him most

9. _____, she was an excellent tennis player.

   (A) Because practiced constantly
   (B) She practiced constantly
   (C) Because practicing constantly
   (D) Because she practiced constantly

10. Social critics often point out the fact that the fast pace of modern life is causing people _____.

   (A) to become increasingly nervous and also even more high-strung
   (B) to become increasingly nervous and high-strung
   (C) to become increasingly nervous and to become increasingly high-strung
   (D) to increasingly become nervous and high-strung

11. That town was no longer the sleepy little village _____.

   (A) it has been being
   (B) it has been
   (C) it was
   (D) it had been

12. If we had known _____, we could have invited him to speak at our ceremonies.

   (A) whom was
   (B) who he was
   (C) who was he
   (D) he was who

13. I will meet you _____.

   (A) of the second floor
   (B) on the floor two
   (C) of the floor two
   (D) on the second floor

14. They were shipwrecked on a tiny island _____.

   (A) off the coast belonging to Japan
   (B) off of the coast of Japan
   (C) off the coast which belongs to Japan
   (D) off the coast of Japan

15. That fire yesterday _____ the whole building.

   (A) could of burned down
   (B) could have burn down
   (C) could burned down
   (D) could have burned down

DIRECTIONS: Blacken the space corresponding to the letter of the *incorrect* part of the sentence (or the one that should be rewritten) on your answer sheet.

16. <u>One</u> should always <u>avoid</u> <u>to change</u> lanes without first <u>signaling</u>.
    A   B   C   D

17. Their custom <u>it</u> is <u>to name</u> the first child <u>after</u> the <u>paternal</u>
             A   B   C   D

grandfather.

18. While <u>staying</u> in Los Angeles, we were able not only <u>to conduct</u>
         A   B

our business but <u>as well as</u> to visit <u>many</u> popular tourist
                   C   D

attractions.

19. Kathy studies very <u>hard</u>, and she <u>is seen</u> <u>in</u> the library
                 A   B C

<u>night and day</u>.
     D

20. Physics is a <u>demanding</u> field that <u>has attracted</u> many people
             A   B

to <u>challenge</u> <u>their</u> complexities.
   C   D

21. The <u>president</u> gave <u>to</u> his advisers the new <u>five-month</u> <u>austerity</u>
      A   B   C   D

plan.

22. The board of directors <u>felt</u> that Clark Weston was <u>more better</u>
                 A   B

suited <u>for</u> the position <u>than</u> William Orly.
     C   D

23. <u>Having lost</u> his job, Edward was <u>only</u> able <u>to finish</u> one semes-
   A   B   C

ter of work before he <u>was forced</u> to leave school.
                  D

24. I <u>cabled</u> <u>them</u> my arrival time <u>so</u> they <u>could meet</u> me at the
     A   B   C   D

    airport.

25. <u>In order to</u> do well <u>on</u> an exam, not only should one know the
       A   B

    required material <u>well</u>, but <u>you</u> should also maintain a relaxed
                  C   D

    attitude.

26. He <u>is said</u> to <u>having been</u> an excellent <u>opera</u> singer <u>in</u> his youth.
      A   B   C   D

27. I <u>have setted</u> the package <u>beside</u> the box of geraniums on the
      A   B

    front porch <u>in case</u> I have to leave before you <u>arrive.</u>
            C   D

28. The coach said <u>that</u> they should <u>have gone</u> to the gym every day
               A   B

    next week <u>to get</u> <u>in shape</u> for the tournament game.
            C   D

29. <u>Having served</u> on that committee <u>for</u> two years, Dr. Anderson is
       A   B

    bored <u>of it</u> and is looking for someone <u>to take</u> his place.
        C   D

30. <u>Jane's</u> decision will probably depend largely <u>to</u> her ability <u>to find</u>
     A   B   C

    a competent person to take care <u>of</u> her young daughter.
                            D

31. <u>A</u> bouquet of beautiful tulips <u>were displayed</u> in an antique vase
    A   B

    <u>on</u> the large mahogany <u>dining-room</u> table.
    C   D

32. He <u>has been</u> the first violinist <u>with</u> the London <u>Philharmonic</u>
      A   B   C

    <u>before</u> he retired ten years ago.
    D

33. Dr. Little is planning on moving (A) to a warmer (B) climate as (C) soon as he will retire (D) next year.

34. The teacher asked them (A) who had completed their tests to turn in (B) their papers and to leave the room as (C) quietly (D) as possible.

35. The native population in the northern part of the country has little (A) opportunities to get (B) the kind (C) of education necessary to compete (D) in modern society.

36. The authorities were (A) determined to discover the (B) identity of the murderer, whom (C) they feared would soon claim another (D) innocent victim.

37. My brother has always helped (A) me in time (B) of need (C), and I wish that he was (D) here now.

38. Their free trip, which (A) they won on (B) a television game show, include (C) four days in London and a (D) week in Paris.

39. I must tell (A) you that you looked so (B) handsomely (C) in your red outfit (D) the other night.

40. A common (A) held (B) belief is that man has evolved (C) from lower forms of (D) life.

Check your answers with the error key on page 245.

XIV

ERROR KEYS FOR PRACTICE TESTS

Test A

ERROR KEY

__A__ 1. (A) Correct
     (B) See *Modifiers—Cause and Result*, page 47.
     (C) Same as A
     (D) Same as A

__C__ 2. (A) See *Modifiers—Demonstratives*, page 34.
     (B) See *Style—Usage*, page 169.
     (C) Correct
     (D) Same as A and B

__C__ 3. (A) See *Style—Correlative Conjunctions*, page 187.
     (B) Same as A
     (C) Correct
     (D) Same as A

__B__ 4. (A) See *Basic Patterns—Clauses*, page 143.
     (B) Correct
     (C) Same as A
     (D) Same as A

__D__ 5. (A) See *Style—Prepositions in Combinations*, page 198.
     (B) Same as A
     (C) Same as A
     (D) Correct

__C__ 6. (A) See *Verbs—Conditionals*, page 82.
     (B) Same as A
     (C) Correct
     (D) Same as A

__B__ 7. (A) See *Modifiers—Too, Very, and Enough*, page 52.
     (B) Correct
     (C) Same as A
     (D) Same as A

_A_ 8. (A) Correct
(B) See *Style—Prepositions in Combinations*, page 198.
(C) Same as B
(D) Same as A. See also *Verbs—Verbals*, page 87.

_B_ 9. (A) See *Pronouns—Personal—Case*, page 109.
(B) Correct
(C) Same as A
(D) Same as A

_B_ 10. (A) See *Pronouns—Faulty Reference*, page 116.
(B) Correct
(C) Same as A. See also *Style—Parallelism*, page 159.
(D) See *Basic Patterns—Order of Adverbs*, page 135.

_D_ 11. (A) See *Verbs—Wishes*, page 80.
(B) Incorrect negative formation (*did not live*)
(C) Same as A
(D) Correct

_B_ 12. (A) See *Style—Wordiness*, page 162.
(B) Correct
(C) Same as A
(D) Same as A. See also *Style—Voice*, page 156.

_A_ 13. (A) Correct
(B) See *Pronouns—Those Modified*, page 122.
(C) Same as B
(D) See *Style—Wordiness*, page 162.

_D_ 14. (A) See *Verbs—Tense*, page 75.
(B) Same as A
(C) Same as A
(D) Correct

_A_ 15. (A) Correct
(B) See *Basic Patterns—To/For (Purpose)*, page 140.
(C) Same as B
(D) Same as B

_D_ 16. (*his* wanting). See *Pronouns—Possessives*, page 114.

_B_ 17. (*lay*). See *Style—Usage*, page 169.

_B_ 18. (these *kinds*). See *Modifiers—Demonstratives*, page 34.

_D_ 19. (*physics*). See *Modifiers—Noun Adjectives*, page 31.

_B_ 20. (*like*). See *Modifiers—Sameness and Similarity*, page 39.

_C_ 21. (*drive*). See *Verbs—Verbals*, page 87.

_B_ 22. (*permanence*). See *Style—Parts of Speech*, page 193.

__B__ 23. (*they finish*). See *Verbs—Time Clauses*, page 77.

__D__ 24. (three-hundred-year-old). See *Modifiers—Hyphenated or Compound Adjectives*, page 33.

__A__ 25. (*Tom had sent*). See *Verbs—Conditionals*, page 82.

__C__ 26. (the *younger*). See *Modifiers—Comparatives*, page 41.

__B__ 27. (*many*). See *Modifiers—Few*, *Little*, *Much*, *and Many*, page 35.

__B__ 28. (*to be* sleeping). See *Verbs—Verbals*, page 87.

__B__ 29. (*an* accurate). See *Modifiers—Articles*, page 50.

__D__ 30. (about the weather *constantly*). See *Basic Patterns—Order of Adverbs*, page 135.

__B__ 31. (*large enough*). See *Modifiers—Too*, *Very*, *and Enough*, page 52.

__C__ 32. (to pay for the cast of my education *completely*). See *Modifiers—Split Infinitives*, page 24.

__C__ 33. (*were not* stationed). See *Verbs—Wishes*, page 80.

__D__ 34. (*the button* broke) OR (*the needle* broke). See *Pronouns—Faulty Reference*, page 116.

__D__ 35. (*it was*). See *Basic Patterns—Embedded Questions*, page 138.

__B__ 36. (*they*). See *Pronouns—Personal—Case*, page 109.

__A__ 37. (having *run*). See *Verbs—Past Participles*, page 91.

__B__ 38. (*no* longer). See *Modifiers—Negation*, page 54.

__A__ 39. (*having*). See *Verbs—Verbals*, page 87.

__B__ 40. (*me*). See *Pronouns—Personal—Case*, page 109.

Test B

ERROR KEY

__D__ 1. (A) See *Basic Patterns—Subject/Verb Agreement*, page 189.
(B) See *Modifiers—Few*, *Little*, *Much*, *and Many*, page 35.
(C) Same as A and B
(D) Correct

__B__ 2. (A) See *Pronouns—Relatives*, page 107.
     (B) Correct
     (C) Same as A
     (D) Same as A

__A__ 3. (A) Correct
     (B) See *Verbs—Tense*, page 75, and *Modifiers—Adjectives after Verbs of Sensation*, page 30.
     (C) Same as B
     (D) See *Verbs—Tense*, page 75.

__C__ 4. (A) See *Modifiers—Noun Adjectives*, page 31.
     (B) Same as A
     (C) Correct
     (D) Same as A

__B__ 5. (A) See *Verbs—Verbals*, page 87.
     (B) Correct
     (C) Same as A
     (D) Same as A

__A__ 6. (A) Correct
     (B) See *Basic Patterns—Indirect Objects*, page 133.
     (C) Same as B
     (D) Same as B

__D__ 7. (A) See *Style—Wordiness*, page 162.
     (B) Same as A
     (C) Same as A
     (D) Correct

__C__ 8. (A) See *Style—Words Often Confused*, GroupI, page 174.
     (B) Same as A. See also *Verbs—Verbs of "Demand,"* page 78, and *Style—Usage*, page 169.
     (C) Correct
     (D) See *Verbs—Verbs of "Demand,"* page 78. See also *Style—Usage* page 169.

__C__ 9. (A) See *Verbs—Modals*, page 85.
     (B) Same as A
     (C) Correct
     (D) Same as A

__C__ 10. (A) See *Basic Patterns—Double Subjects*, page 141.
     (B) See *Basic Patterns—Clauses*, page 142.
     (C) Correct
     (D) Same as B

__C__ 11. (A) See *Style—Parallelism*, page 159.
     (B) Same as A
     (C) Correct
     (D) Same as A

<u>A</u> 12. (A) Correct
    (B) See *Verbs—Verbs of "Demand"*, page 78.
    (C) Same as B
    (D) Same as B

<u>C</u> 13. (A) See *Modifiers—Comparatives*, page 41.
    (B) Same as A
    (C) Correct
    (D) Same as A

<u>D</u> 14. (A) See *Modifiers—Adjective/Adverb Confusion*, page 27.
    (B) See *Verbs—Conditionals*, page 82.
    (C) See *Modifiers—Comparatives*, page 41.
    (D) Correct

<u>C</u> 15. (A) See *Pronouns—Number*, page 119.
    (B) See *Pronouns—Person*, page 117.
    (C) Correct
    (D) Same as C

<u>A</u> 16. (*lost respect*). See *Modifiers—Articles*, page 50.

<u>A</u> 17 (*whether*). See *Style—Words Often Confused*, Group III, page 184.

<u>D</u> 18. (might *have* enjoyed). See *Verbs—Conditionals*, page 82.

<u>A</u> 19. (*Since Howard did not pass the law exam,*). See *Modifiers—Dangling Modifiers*, page 25.

<u>A</u> 20. (*interestingly*). See *Modifiers—Adjective/Adverb Confusion*, page 27.

<u>D</u> 21. (*anywhere*). See *Style—Substandard*, page 166.

<u>A</u> 22. (*I reserved*). See *Verbs—Tense*, page 75.

<u>C</u> 23. (*and an*). See *Style—Parallelism*, page 159.

<u>D</u> 24. (*without rain*). See *Modifiers—Negation*, page 54.

<u>A</u> 25. (such a difficult time). See *Modifiers—Cause and Result*, page 47.

<u>B</u> 26. (*make*). See *Verbs—Verbals*, page 87.

<u>C</u> 27. (*whoever*). See *Pronouns—<u>Who</u>/<u>Whom</u>*, page 111.

<u>A</u> 28. (*between*). See *Style—Usage*, page 169.

<u>A</u> 29. (*who*). See *Pronouns—Relatives*, page 107.

<u>A</u> 30. (*these*). See *Modifiers—Demonstratives*, page 34.

<u>D</u> 31. (*Henry's*). See *Modifiers—Comparatives*, page 41.

__C__ 32. (*to catch*). See *Basic Patterns—To/For (Purpose)*, page 140.

__B__ 33. (*so* satisfying). See *Modifiers—Cause and Result*, page 47.

__C__ 34. (*gate one*). See *Modifiers—Cardinal and Ordinal Numbers*, page 38.

__B__ 35. (*has risen*). See *Style—Usage*, page 169.

__B__ 36. (*turn off*). See *Verbs—Verbs of "Demand,"* page 78.

__B__ 37. (*quite*). See *Style—Words Often Confused*, Group II, page 179.

__A__ 38. (*tired*). See *Modifiers—Adjectives after Verbs of Sensation*, page 30.

__C__ 39. (*still* has not returned). See *Basic Patterns—Order of Adverbs*, page 135.

__C__ 40. (*sat*). See *Style—Usage*, page 169.

Test C

ERROR KEY

__B__ 1. (A) See *Pronouns—Number*, page 119.
    (B) Correct
    (C) See *Pronouns—Person*, page 117.
    (D) Same as C

__A__ 2. (A) Correct
    (B) See *Modifiers—Negation*, page 54.
    (C) See *Modifiers—Articles*, page 50.
    (D) See *Verbs—Present and Perfect Participles and Infinitives,* page 94.

__D__ 3. (A) See *Modifiers—Adverbs like Only*, page 23.
    (B) See *Modifiers—Split Infinitives*, page 24.
    (C) Same as A
    (D) Correct

__C__ 4. (A) See *Style—Substandard*, page 166.
    (B) Same as A
    (C) Correct
    (D) Same as A

__D__ 5. (A) See *Basic Patterns—Embedded Questions*, page 138.
    (B) Same as A
    (C) Same as A
    (D) Correct

__B__ 6. (A) See *Modifiers—Split Infinitives*, page 24.
     (B) Correct
     (C) See *Basic Patterns—Order of Adverbs*, page 135.
     (D) Same as C

__C__ 7. (A) See *Modifiers—Comparatives*, page 41.
     (B) See *Style—Parallelism*, page 159.
     (C) Correct
     (D) Same as A and B.

__A__ 8. (A) Correct
     (B) See *Wordiness*, page 162.
     (C) See *Style—Voice*, page 156.
     (D) Same as B

__D__ 9. (A) See *Basic Patterns—Clauses*, page 144.
     (B) Same as A
     (C) Same as A
     (D) Correct

__B__ 10. (A) See *Style—Wordiness*, page 162.
     (B) Correct
     (C) Same as A
     (D) See *Modifiers—Split Infinitives*, page 24.

__D__ 11. (A) See *Verbs—Tense*, page 75.
     (B) Same as A
     (C) Same as A
     (D) Correct

__B__ 12. (A) See *Pronouns—Who/Whom*, page 111.
     (B) Correct
     (C) See *Basic Patterns—Embedded Questions*, page 138.
     (D) Same as C

__D__ 13. (A) See *Style—Prepositions (General Use)*, page 195.
     (B) See *Modifiers—Cardinal and Ordinal Numbers*, page 38.
     (C) Same as A and B
     (D) Correct

__D__ 14. (A) See *Style—Wordiness*, page 162.
     (B) See *Style—Substandard*, page 166.
     (C) See *Style—Wordiness*, page 162.
     (D) Correct

__D__ 15. (A) See *Verbs—Modals*, page 85.
     (B) See *Verbs—Past Participles*, page 91.
     (C) Same as A
     (D) Correct

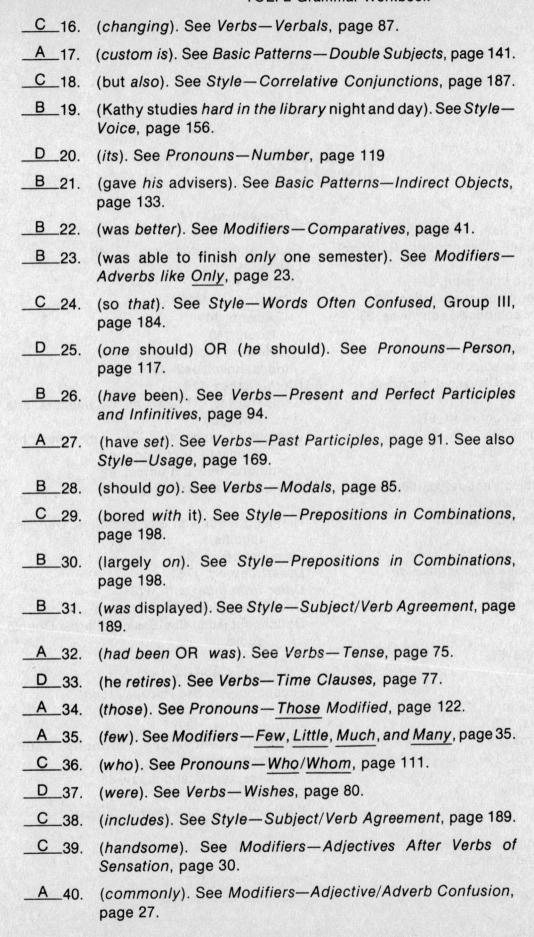

C 16. (*changing*). See *Verbs—Verbals*, page 87.

A 17. (*custom is*). See *Basic Patterns—Double Subjects*, page 141.

C 18. (but *also*). See *Style—Correlative Conjunctions*, page 187.

B 19. (Kathy studies *hard in the library* night and day). See *Style—Voice*, page 156.

D 20. (*its*). See *Pronouns—Number*, page 119

B 21. (gave *his* advisers). See *Basic Patterns—Indirect Objects*, page 133.

B 22. (was *better*). See *Modifiers—Comparatives*, page 41.

B 23. (was able to finish *only* one semester). See *Modifiers—Adverbs like Only*, page 23.

C 24. (so *that*). See *Style—Words Often Confused*, Group III, page 184.

D 25. (*one* should) OR (*he* should). See *Pronouns—Person*, page 117.

B 26. (*have* been). See *Verbs—Present and Perfect Participles and Infinitives*, page 94.

A 27. (have *set*). See *Verbs—Past Participles*, page 91. See also *Style—Usage*, page 169.

B 28. (should *go*). See *Verbs—Modals*, page 85.

C 29. (bored *with* it). See *Style—Prepositions in Combinations*, page 198.

B 30. (largely *on*). See *Style—Prepositions in Combinations*, page 198.

B 31. (*was* displayed). See *Style—Subject/Verb Agreement*, page 189.

A 32. (*had been* OR *was*). See *Verbs—Tense*, page 75.

D 33. (he *retires*). See *Verbs—Time Clauses*, page 77.

A 34. (*those*). See *Pronouns—Those Modified*, page 122.

A 35. (*few*). See *Modifiers—Few, Little, Much, and Many*, page 35.

C 36. (*who*). See *Pronouns—Who/Whom*, page 111.

D 37. (*were*). See *Verbs—Wishes*, page 80.

C 38. (*includes*). See *Style—Subject/Verb Agreement*, page 189.

C 39. (*handsome*). See *Modifiers—Adjectives After Verbs of Sensation*, page 30.

A 40. (*commonly*). See *Modifiers—Adjective/Adverb Confusion*, page 27.

INDEX